"*Rembrandts in the Attic* is a seminal book about a vital but often forgotten topic. Read it, and you'll never again think about patents in the same way."

—*Gil Amelio, Founder, AmTech, LLC; former CEO, Apple Computer and National Semiconductor*

"Intellectual capital, such as patents, is the fuel that powers innovation. *Rembrandts in the Attic* is a must-read for any CEO interested in innovation and intellectual capital."

—*Bob Howe, CEO, Scient*

"Like it or not, patents have become a major force in business. Rivette and Kline illustrate the importance of senior-level management's involvement in the intellectual property strategy of a successful corporation, and present a road map to a solid patent strategy."

—*Rich Belgard, Columnist, "PatentWatch"*

"*Rembrandts in the Attic* is prerequisite reading for investors and managers of high-technology companies. Rivette and Kline present a convincing case for why managing patents will become increasingly important with the growth of knowledge-based economies."

—*Bob Barrett, Founding Partner, Battery Venture*

"Fully 76 percent of the Fortune 100's total market capitalization is represented by intangible assets, such as patents, copyrights, and trademarks. Yet corporations still focus their attention on tangibles. *Rembrandts in the Attic* provides deep and actionable insight into how leading corporations are managing and extracting value from the most tangible of the intangibles—patents."

—*Peter J. King, Managing Partner, Arthur Andersen's Intellectual Property Asset Management Practice*

REMBRANDTS
IN THE ATTIC

REMBRANDTS
IN THE ATTIC

Unlocking the Hidden
Value of Patents

KEVIN G. RIVETTE
DAVID KLINE

Harvard Business School Press
Boston, Massachusetts

ThemeScape is a registered trademark of Cartia, Inc.

Library of Congress Cataloging-in-Publication Data

Rivette, Kevin G., 1956–
    Rembrandts in the attic : unlocking the hidden value of patents /
    Kevin G. Rivette, David Kline.
        p.   cm.
    ISBN 0-87584-899-0 (alk. paper)
    1. Patents.   I. Kline, David, 1950–   .   II. Title.
T211.R58 2000
608.773—dc21   99-33756
                                                                        CIP

The paper used in this publication meets the requirements of the
American National Standard for Permanence of Paper for Publications and Documents in Libraries and Archives Z39.48-1992.

To Dorothy, for always believing in me,

And with special love to Spencer, Elizabeth, and Lisa.

Kevin G. Rivette

To Sarah, whose patient love has reawakened me to life's sweet and spicy possibilities,

And to my son Daniel, whose cool wit and warm heart inspire me.

David Kline

CONTENTS

PREFACE

What did the ex-patent lawyer say to the ex-war correspondent?

No, this is not another lawyer joke. It's actually the very first question I asked Kevin Rivette on that blustery winter day in January 1998 when I sat across a Silicon Valley lunch table from him and listened to his proposal.

"I'm sorry—what did you say?" were my exact words, if I recall. "You want me to help you write a book about *what?*"

"Patents," Kevin nodded eagerly.

Frankly, I found it difficult to share his enthusiasm. As a former war correspondent who spent ten years hiking into war zones, I had come to expect a little high-stakes excitement, a certain dramatic heft, to the stories I wrote about. Even after I finally figured out (genius that I am) that maybe I ought to find something safer to do—I switched "beats" in 1992 from the battlefields of war to those of business—I still took pride in my ability to tell a good war story, even if it now involved opposing companies instead of armies. So you can imagine my reaction at being asked to devote the next two years of my life to co-writing a book about a subject that most people (myself included) considered to be quite possibly the most boring on earth.

I turned him down flat. And then two more times over the next few months as well—Kevin Rivette is nothing if not persistent—I turned him down again. But as anyone who knows Kevin can attest, he is unstoppable when motivated by a vision. And in this case, not only did he have a vision, he also had no intention of letting my initial obstinacy get in the way of me ultimately helping him realize that vision.

So with a patient dedication to softening me up that reminded me of a dog with a bone, Kevin started chewing away at my resistance. We had several meetings, during which he told me his story. Before becoming an entrepreneur, he explained, he had been a patent attorney and had come to appreciate the rich mother lode of intelligence that a company could glean about its competitors' strategies from publicly available patent filings. But most businesses ignored this gold mine of patent data—"the greatest source of competitive intelligence on earth," he called it—in part because they failed to grasp just how valuable intellectual property had become as financial assets and competitive weapons in today's knowledge economy. This corporate neglect of the *business* (as opposed to strictly legal) uses of patents also stemmed from the enormous cost and difficulty that had always been associated with trying to mine patent data for competitive advantage.

Only a few years ago, in fact, a company might have spent six to nine months laboriously pouring over reams of paper documents just trying to "patent map" one competitor's product development plans and capabilities. But now, new data-mining and visualization technologies made it possible for this same firm to accomplish the task in days or even hours—and then to develop patent strategies of its own to outflank and block that competitor, solidify its own proprietary market advantage, safeguard its future technology leadership, and enhance its overall commercial success.

Think of it, Kevin suggested, like those World War II–era

advances in long-range bomber and aircraft carrier design that enabled nations for the first time to project their air power anywhere on earth. (And a crafty suggestion it was, too, for he had discovered that we shared a mutual lifelong interest in World War II military history.) Just as those new bomber and carrier designs had transformed air power from a merely tactical into a truly strategic weapon of war, so had today's new data-mining and visualization tools enabled patents and other intellectual property to be systematically deployed for the first time as strategic weapons of business competition—if, that is, you knew how to do so.

And therein lay Kevin Rivette's vision: he wanted us to write the first popular business book that actually showed CEOs and other senior managers how to develop and deploy patent strategies for competitive advantage.

The book, he said, should be a primer on the next great corporate challenge: developing new tactics, new strategies, for the new competitive battlefields of the knowledge economy. Patents would be the "smart" bombs of tomorrow's business wars. And together we could show companies precisely how to aim them to achieve competitive victory.

Like I said, I'm a sucker for a good war story.

David Kline
September 1, 1999

ACKNOWLEDGMENTS

All books are collaborative efforts, but this one is especially so. Indeed, to even attempt to write a book that breaks ground in an entirely new frontier of corporate strategy development requires much more in the way of advice and counsel, criticism, and support than the casual reader might suppose.

Among the many chief executives, senior managers, corporate counsels, entrepreneurs, business strategy consultants, industry analysts, investment bankers, venture capitalists, journalists, technologists, software designers, patent experts, policy makers, and economists who gave so generously of their time and wisdom to this project, we wish to thank in particular (and in alphabetical order) the following:

Sydney Alpert, Gil Amelio, Bob Barrett, Richard Belgard, David Bradford, David Brodwin, H. Lee Browne, Daniel Burstein, John Bush, John Cioffi, Peter Detkin, Eugene Emmerich, Stephen Fox, Henry Garrana, Dan Giannini, Aaron Goldberg, Nat Goldhaber, Robert Goldscheider, Ken Hao, Steve Hopkins, Takeshi Isayama, Jan Jaferian, Sam Khoury, Jerry Klein, Mark Leiberman, Andrew Leonard, David Leonard, John Mathon, former Commissioner of Patents and Trademarks Gerald R. Mossinghoff, Mark Myers, Cynthia O'Donohue, Ray Ozzie, Ethan Penner, Bruce Perens, former U.S. Secretary of Commerce Peter G. Peterson, David Pullman, Eric Raymond, Paul Romer, Steve Rowe, Rebecca Runkle, Mel Sharpe, Steve Slater, Jerry Stanley, Robert Green Sterne, Anthony Stoss, G. Richard Thoman, Alberto Torres, and Paul Turner. Since we interviewed these people directly, their statements are not referenced by endnotes in the book.

We thank also the many people at Aurigin Systems, Inc., whose editorial input and support greatly strengthened this book, including Luke Hohmann (an author himself), Dan'l Lewin, Larry Caddy, Irving Rappaport, Paul Germeraad, Steve Dobbs, and Chris Benham. Special thanks to Scott Malcolm for designing the charts and other graphic visualizations of competitive patent analysis that make this book so useful and unique.

In addition to all those above, we wish to express our special appreciation to our editor at Harvard Business School Press, Hollis Heimbouch. It is rare that authors have the luck and privilege of working with an editor who truly brings out the best in them. Hollis Heimbouch's patient support and wise counsel made this a far better book than it otherwise might have been, and we owe her a great debt of gratitude for that.

We also cannot allow to pass unnoticed the contributions of the other members of the Harvard Business School Press team, including Genoveva Llosa, Barbara Roth, Gayle Treadwell, Sarah McConville, Charles Dresner, Ellen McCullough, Ellen Chase, Leslie Zheutlin, and Maryanne Spillane. Their efforts ensured that the book would not only be well-designed and readable, but that it would also be widely read.

We come now to the one individual without whose help we can quite safely say this book would not exist. Elisabeth Feldman's extraordinary contributions defy easy classification: she was both researcher and muse, critic and therapist, devil's advocate and beta tester of many of the most compelling conceptual breakthroughs in this book. In a just world, her name would be featured on the jacket alongside ours.

Finally, we want to thank our families and friends for their patient support during our arduous two-year-long effort to write this book. We offer our special love and appreciation to our mothers, Patricia Rivette and Ruth Rothman, because God knows mothers never really get the thanks they deserve, do they?

THE NEW COMPETITIVE
BATTLEFIELD

This book is about intellectual property (IP), once considered the most boring subject in the world. Until very recently, in fact, simply mentioning the words *patents* or *intellectual property* at a social gathering was guaranteed to invite blank stares, followed by an awkward shuffling of feet as everyone suddenly spotted dear old friends that he or she simply *had* to go talk to. Today, patent lawyers attract small crowds at parties—rather like astrologers used to and plastic surgeons still do—and find themselves peppered with questions such as whether that wonderful idea for a bird diaper is patentable (the answer is yes—it was issued Patent No. 2,882,858).

What changed? Quite simply, the world did. The old industrial era has been supplanted by a new knowledge-based economy in which ideas and innovation rather than land or natural resources have become the principal

1

wellsprings of economic growth and competitive business advantage. And because the economic forces that structure our daily lives are so different today than they were even a generation ago, it is only natural that we perceive the sources and nature of value very differently as well.

Remember when ideas were a dime a dozen—indeed, "no better than dreams," said Emerson, unless forged by "the arms of good and brave men" into something tangible? And who can forget the tragedy of *Death of a Salesman*'s Willy Loman, desperately chasing his elusive "one-million-dollar idea"? Today, however, the *Wall Street Journal* features stories such as "Big Idea Turns Priceline's Founder into a Billionaire," which profiles the entrepreneur Jay Walker—a "collector of ideas," the paper called him approvingly—whose business consists for the most part simply of thinking up *ideas* for new businesses.[1] And all across America, inventors who once tried to build better mousetraps today nurture the hope simply of coming up with an idea for one.

Without patents, the future of your business may be owned by someone else.

In an age when ideas themselves command enormous value, it is hardly surprising that the rights to ownership of these ideas have now become a matter of intense policy debate, legal argument, and competitive jockeying by businesses. While this book will touch on some of the legal and policy debates surrounding patents, for the most part we have restricted our discussion to their actual role and uses in the world of business today. We have concentrated, in other words, on the world as it *is*, not as it (perhaps) ought to be.

And in the world as it is, observes the *New York Times*, "Intellectual property [has been] transformed from a sleepy area of law and business to one of the driving engines of a high-technology economy."[2] Indeed, the competitive battles once fought for control of markets and raw materials are now increasingly being waged over the exclusive rights to new ideas and inventions. Whereas executives once feared that competitors might outproduce or outmarket them, today they worry that rivals—especially in the booming e-commerce industries of the Internet—may secure the patent rights to the essential technologies or even to the fundamental business concepts that they need in order to be in business in the first place.

As one commentator warned, "Companies that don't claim their stake in the future will wake up and discover that their competitors own all the patents they need to be on the Web."[3]

To be sure, only a minority of American businesses even have an intellectual property strategy, and they are usually reluctant to talk about it for fear of letting rivals in on what they consider to be their secret weapon. But we've managed to pierce the veil of secrecy shrouding the use of patents in business today. We'll show how some of the world's most successful companies—market leaders such as Intel and Microsoft, Lucent and Xerox, IBM and Web start-up Priceline.com— have begun using their patents as competitive weapons to capture and defend markets, outflank rivals, and increase revenue. These firms regard patent strategy as a new core competency of the modern enterprise and an important factor in their success.

The vast majority of companies, however, are simply unaware of the often-enormous economic and competitive values that lie untapped within their patent portfolios. In fact, some firms are opposed to the competitive use of patents altogether, fearing an IP arms race that only the biggest corporations can afford to win. We address this concern later in this chapter.

Whatever your view of patents, this much is clear: firms ignore their growing power in business today only at their peril.

Welcome to the new competitive battlefield: intellectual property.

THE PATENT RACE IS ON

"Open a newspaper, surf the Web, patent disputes and agreements are everywhere," observes *Forbes* magazine. "If ever there were a field with financial opportunity written all over it, it would have to be the fusty musty world of patents."[4]

Indeed, patent activity is mushrooming across virtually every sector of the U.S. economy as companies seek to gain a proprietary market advantage, an exclusive hold over a new technology, or an opportunity to tap new revenues. The number of new U.S. patents issued in 1998 reached nearly 155,000—a 33 percent increase over 1997, and more than two and one-half times the level that prevailed throughout most of this century (see Figure 1-1a). A decade ago, Microsoft had one patent; today it has close to 800. Sun, Oracle, Novell, Dell, and Intel have likewise boosted the size of their patent portfolios by more than 500 percent just in the last few years (see Figure 1-1b).

FIGURE 1-1a   NEW PATENTS ISSUED ANNUALLY, 1980–1998

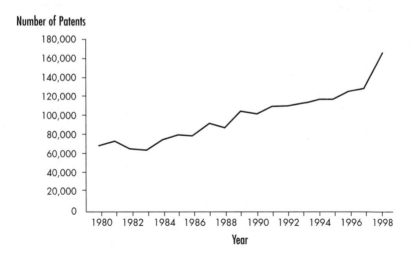

Source: Courtesy of Aurigin Systems, Inc.

Along with this explosion of patents has come a boom in the revenues derived from patent licensing, as companies realize that intellectual property is among their most valuable and fungible of assets. Patent licensing revenues have shot up 700 percent in the past eight years alone, from $15 billion in 1990 to well over $100 billion in 1998 (see Figure 1-1c). And experts point out that the licensing market is still only in its infancy. Revenues, they say, could top a half-trillion dollars annually by the middle of the next decade.

Intellectual property has also served as the hidden motive behind a number of the biggest corporate mergers of recent years, including the surprise $10 billion acquisition of Netscape by America Online. In that deal, many analysts wondered why Sun Microsystems had joined in the acquisition of Netscape, for Sun's costs in the deal appeared greater than the $500 million worth of Internet servers that AOL had promised to buy from

FIGURE 1-1b   HIGH-TECH COMPANY PATENTS OWNED, 1994–1998

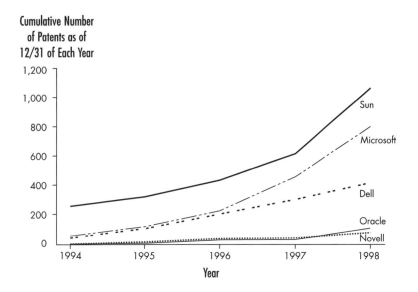

Cumulative Number of Patents as of 12/31 of Each Year

Sun. The real reason? "What really got us going was the ability to control [Netscape's] intellectual property," explains Sun's Chief Operating Officer Ed Zander. "That's the key [to] what got us intrigued."[5] A Goldman Sachs research report concurred: "What Sun is paying for, in essence, is intellectual property (IP). With this accord, Sun is able to get key [software] that it has been missing [that] could have cost upwards of $1 billion plus a considerable amount of time to have developed internally."[6]

Billions at Stake in E-Commerce Patent Rights

Nowhere is the frenzy over patent rights more intense, however, than in the emerging electronic commerce industries of the Internet, where entrepreneurs are rushing to stake their proprietary claims to this booming new frontier of business. "A Flood of

---

FIGURE 1-1c   PATENT LICENSING REVENUES, 1980–1999

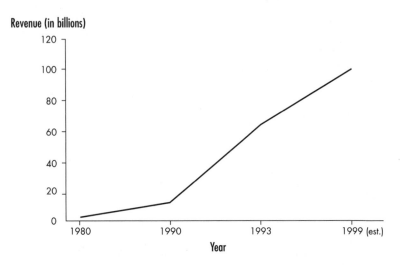

Sources: *The Economist*, 22 August 1992, 56; Fred Warshofsky, *The Patent Wars: The Battle to Own the World's Technology* (New York: Wiley, 1994), 30. Courtesy of Aurigin Systems, Inc.

New Web Patents," "E-Commerce Companies Wield Patents in Fight for Competitive Edge," "Web Patent Bonanza!"—the headlines testify to the fear and frenzy over e-commerce patent rights. And the on-line battle over intellectual property has barely even begun. Many of the most fundamental e-commerce patents, especially the more controversial ones that cover methods of doing business, are still pending and won't be issued until late 1999 or the year 2000.

What's more, there's a new wildcard in the intensifying e-commerce patent wars: the Open Source movement, a worldwide confederation of volunteer software developers whose nonproprietary software forms the infrastructure of the Net. Shunning intellectual property rights altogether, the Open Source movement represents a significant challenge to the traditional use of patents within business. In Chapter 7, we show why and how companies must adapt their patent strategies to meet the Open Source challenge—to the benefit and profit of both.

As *Forbes* put it, "There's a lot of money at stake here. And more to come as the technology sector continues to drive the American economy."[7]

It's not just the American economy that is affected by these trends, either. Patent activity is on the rise worldwide, with international patent applications jumping by 23 percent in 1998—including, for the first time, patents from inventors in Azerbaijan, Vietnam, and Zimbabwe. This increase in global patenting is spurred in part by the World Trade Organization's (WTO) Agreement on Trade-Related Aspects of Intellectual Property Rights (TRIPS), which requires most WTO member nations to reform and strengthen their intellectual property laws by the year 2000. As one Japanese trade official put it, "The Year 2000 will be the real opening of the era of intellectual property rights."[8]

In Japan, however, intellectual property reform is much more than a trade issue. It's also seen as a key component of efforts to overcome bureaucracy and kick-start the Japanese economy. Listen to Japanese Patent Office commissioner Takeshi Isayama: "Because of Japan's [economic troubles], the country's intellectual property has grown in importance. Inventions and patents by nature lead to innovation. Therefore, Japan intends to establish strong and broad intellectual property rights, create a market for the trading of patents [and] work towards the development of corporate global competition based on intellectual property rights." One of the specific reforms outlined by Isayama is especially noteworthy for *keiretsu*-dominated Japan. "Those launching new businesses such as venture companies and those intending to increase intellectual property," says Isayama, "will be afforded various preferential treatments."[9]

As a former Japanese patent examiner put it, "Japan has no natural resources. Intellectual properties are the only asset we have." [10]

A New Business Driver Emerges

Here at home, meanwhile, intellectual property is also having an effect on new business formation and the capital markets, as start-up firms seeking capital discover that their chances of being funded are much greater if they have patent protection for their risky new ventures. Jay Walker's Priceline.com is a case in point. The company, which runs an auction business on the Web, gained national notoriety in the summer of 1998 when it won a patent for its method of doing business—a buyer-driven form of electronic auction. Having such a broad patent, says Walker, was crucial not only in attracting former Citicorp president Richard Braddock as the firm's CEO, but also in raising venture funding for the firm to the tune of $100 million—an almost unprecedented amount for a young Internet start-up.

Moreover, entirely new kinds of businesses are being formed

in which intellectual property itself is the raison d'être for the venture. Patent development firms, intellectual property licensing enterprises, even trading exchanges for patent licenses—there's plenty of money to be made when the "product" itself is intellectual property. Walker Digital, for example, is Priceline.com's parent company and an "intellectual property laboratory" that has created over 200 patentable business ideas that will be licensed or spun off into new companies. "We benefit our shareholders by building a portfolio of intellectual property that other companies can use to grow their businesses," explains Jay Walker.[11]

Another example is Yet2.com, an intellectual property marketplace for the licensing and sale of technology patents that is slated to launch in late 1999. Yet2.com hopes to garner a critical mass of intellectual properties through agreements it has forged with such leading technology companies as 3M, Allied-Signal, Boeing, Dow, Dupont, Ford, Honeywell, Polaroid, and Rockwell to contribute technologies to the exchange. Whether or not Yet2.com actually succeeds in creating a viable IP trading market, other attempts are being contemplated—including one called the Patent & License Exchange.

Intellectual property management has become a new corporate strategy issue.

Or consider the case of Real3D, a company created entirely out of Lockheed-Martin's patent portfolio. Seeing more than a little market potential for its underutilized flight simulator technology patents, the aerospace firm spun off the company in 1997, and it quickly secured $65 million in investment from Intel and Silicon Graphics. Today the company has a market value of "several hundred million dollars," according to Hambrecht & Quist analyst Ken Hao—all based, apparently, on the company's patents, since it has no products yet.

Patent portfolios, in fact, are even starting to be used as

investment instruments. In the first-ever use of patents as vehicles for off-balance-sheet financing, Global Asset Capital, a San Francisco–based investment banking boutique, announced in January 1999 that it planned to securitize the future royalties of drug company patent portfolios and sell the notes to investors.[12] Two months later, the first conference on IP asset securitization was held in New York City, attended by leading investment banks. According to conference organizers, "Securitizing and valuing intellectual property are the hottest balance-sheet topics in the marketplace."[13]

Says prominent Washington, D.C., patent attorney Robert Green Sterne: "Patents are having a major impact on financing. The investment banking community, the venture capital community, and the angel investing community are very interested in intellectual property."[14]

No Patents on Wall Street?

Even the old saw about there being "no patents on Wall Street" has now gone the way of the passbook savings account. On July 23, 1998, the Federal Circuit U.S. Court of Appeals set a major new precedent when it upheld the patentability of Signature Financial Group's "hub-and-spoke" system, which enables multiple mutual funds (the "spokes") to pool their assets into a single portfolio fund (the "hub") for investing, thereby generating both economies of scale in administering the fund as well as the tax advantages of a partnership. With this ruling, the court established for the first time the principle that trading practices and investment strategies could be patented. And it settled once and for all the debate that has raged for 18 years—ever since Merrill Lynch received a patent in 1982 for its cash-management account—over whether there is, indeed, a place for patents on Wall Street.

The decision naturally sent shock waves throughout the financial community. "Patent War on Wall Street!" screamed one headline. *Business Week* complained, "What's Next—A Patent for the 401(k)?" But like it or not, warned one report, the ruling is sure to force "an immediate re-evaluation of the intellectual property strategy of every major company in the banking, insurance, and financial industries doing business in the United States."[15]

Patent Asset Management: A New Corporate Strategy Issue

Capital formation and asset exploitation, of course, are major strategy issues for CEOs, so it's no surprise that management consulting firms have begun to devote considerable resources to helping Fortune 1000 clients develop IP management capabilities. When Coopers & Lybrand (since merged with Price Waterhouse to form PriceWaterhouseCoopers) announced its new IP management practice in late 1997, it noted that globalization, shortened product life cycles, and the high rate of technological change "pressure high tech companies to take a closer look at exploiting and protecting their intellectual property rights. Yet many companies are completely unaware of [their] true value and potential competitive advantage."[16]

Not any more. The research and consulting firm Delphi Group reports that 75 percent of businesses surveyed identify intellectual asset management as a new corporate strategy issue.[17] And according to PriceWaterhouseCoopers partner Aron Levko, who manages that firm's Intellectual Asset Management Practice, "Companies are taking the first steps to organize the disparate pieces of their intellectual assets" in order to transform these into "engines of corporate growth."[18] Even allowing for a certain amount of exaggeration born of self-interest, it is clear that the management of patent assets is becoming a major new strategy challenge for corporate America. In addition to the firms mentioned previously, Arthur Andersen, Arthur D. Little, McKinsey & Co., KPMG Peat Marwick, and Deloitte & Touche are also launching IP management practices.

From Academia to the Law: Patents Mean Business

Intellectual property asset exploitation has also become a hot topic in the halls of academia, a realm that generated $611 million in licensing fees from university-owned patents in 1997—an 89 percent jump over 1993. University patents also helped jumpstart 333 new entrepreneurial ventures that year. Debates rage, of course, over the potential conflict of interest between academic freedom and the desire to profit from the research fruits of that freedom. But however these conflicts are ultimately resolved, universities are unlikely to go back to the days when research ideas were regarded solely as items of academic, and not also economic, interest.

Meanwhile, never ones to ignore a potential profit (or, for that matter, a potential loss), insurance companies have also gotten into the act. Dallas, Texas–based Summit Global Partners has joined with underwriters Lloyd's of London to offer coverage against patent infringement lawsuits. "There are thousands of new companies that are creating all sorts of new products, and many are being challenged on the grounds that they have infringed on someone else's patent," explains Summit Global's managing partner for intellectual property risk management, Ronald Reshefsky, who expects such coverage to also help firms attract venture and other investors. "Until now, there was no way to offer these companies real protection for their balance sheets." [19]

Wherever money goes, of course, so go the lawyers. Hence even the legal profession has been caught up in the pandemonium over patents. Intellectual property lawyers are now the fastest-growing specialty in law (just try to find an out-of-work patent attorney!) and one of the "10 hottest jobs in Silicon Valley," according to the *San Jose Mercury News*.[20] And although lawyers are hardly known for pushing the envelope of services to clients, pressure from corporate clients is clearly forcing IP lawyers to abandon their strictly legalistic approach to patents. At a 1999 meeting of the American Intellectual Property Lawyers Association (AIPLA), for example, the usual thrilling discussions of such heart-stopping legal arcana as the doctrine of equivalents (don't ask—it even puts patent lawyers to sleep!) were hardly in evidence. Instead, the AIPLA held workshops on "maximizing return on intellectual assets," "turning the patent portfolio into a profit-making venture," and "using patent portfolios to achieve business objectives."

THE DEBATE OVER PATENTS

In short, just about everyone is talking about intellectual property, but not all the talk is favorable. Concerns have been raised about recent trends in patent activity—the patenting of business methods and other abstract concepts, for example, as well as the proliferation of bogus "trash" patents—that some believe are having a chilling effect on innovation and the development of the new e-commerce industries of the Internet. In fact, some critics argue that rather than promoting innovation, today's patent gold rush is actually fostering an IP arms race that will eventually enable firms with large patent arsenals to monopolize entire technology sectors and then use the threat of infringement suits to bludgeon smaller, more innovative firms into competitive submission.

Viewing Patents in Historical Context

Before addressing such concerns, however, it's important to view today's patent activity in its proper context. For when measured against previous patent cycles in U.S. history, it is remarkable how *unremarkable* the current patenting stampede actually is.

As you can see from Figure 1-2, the United States has witnessed several similar upsurges of patenting in its history. The first one occurred during the time of Alexander Graham Bell and Thomas Edison in the 1880s, when the average number of new patents issued each year jumped 56 percent, to about 20,000, compared with the 12,000 patents issued yearly the previous decade. This patent boom corresponded, of course, with rapid advances in the emerging steam, railroad, telegraph, telephone, and electric power industries that signaled the industrialization of the U.S. economy. The next big increase in patent issuances began around 1902 and lasted until 1916 or so, when the number of patents granted doubled from 20,000 per year to around 40,000 annually. This was the period of the newborn automobile and aircraft industries' most rapid early-stage growth. Patenting levels then remained relatively stable at about 40,000 per year until around 1960 or so, when the revolution in plastics and other synthetic materials along with boom-time growth in the aerospace and computer industries pushed patenting levels to 60,000 per year. And there they remained until the mid-1980s, when the personal computer and other emerging high-tech industries of Silicon Valley began to power the whole of the

FIGURE 1-2 U.S. PATENTS ISSUED, 1850–1998

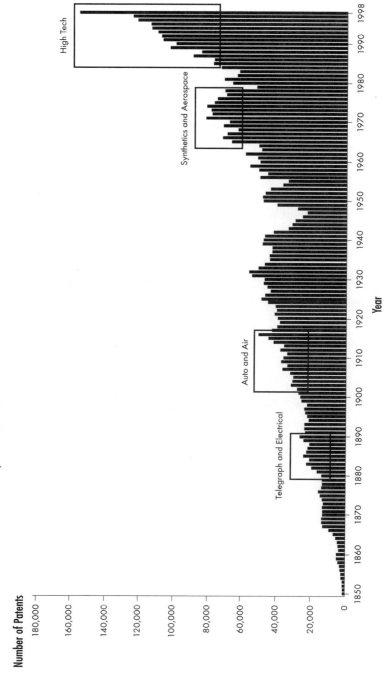

American economy and propel us steadily toward the age of the Internet.

Clearly, whenever the United States has undergone a major industrial renaissance during which technology advances led not only to the birth of new industries but to the reshaping of existing ones, patenting levels have risen dramatically. It is precisely such an economy-transforming renaissance that we are witnessing today.

Can You Patent Ideas?

Although the increase in patenting itself may not be all that unusual, the nature of what is being patented in some cases is. Particularly controversial are recent patents not for devices or other tangible inventions but for technology-enabled methods of doing business. Indeed, ever since the U.S. Supreme Court in January 1999 affirmed the court decision referred to earlier (*State Street Bank v. Signature Financial Group*) that software-enabled business processes are indeed patentable so long as these are novel, nonobvious, and produce tangible results, the patenting of business models, marketing strategies, and other abstract innovations has mushroomed.

Some comdemn this trend, warning that the patenting of business methods may eventually lead to the monopolization of entire areas of conceptual knowledge and to the stifling of academic freedom, scientific inquiry, and technological innovation. To illustrate their case, these critics often pose a future scenario in which someone patents not a better mousetrap but simply the *idea* of catching mice. Presumably, the patentee would then be able to block anyone else from catching mice—at least for the 20-year term of the patent—unless he or she receives a royalty.

There are several things wrong with this scenario, not the least of which is that Patent and Trademark Office (PTO) rules dictate that the idea of catching mice is clearly *not* patentable because it is neither novel nor nonobvious. And even if the idea of catching mice were novel, it would still require an enabling technology component to be patentable. The same is true for such mundane business methods as selling door to door or franchising.

Exaggerated scenarios aside, the real heart of the debate is whether it is appropriate in our knowledge-based economy to view nonphysical or intangible inventions as patentable subject matter. Once again, the issues become clearer when viewed in historical context. The history of economic progress on our planet, after all, is essentially the story of humanity's long climb up the ladder of abstraction—from brute force to the subtle use of energy, from resource-based wealth to wealth derived from ever more creative ideas about how to use those resources. Isn't it only logical, therefore, to expect that invention itself should follow a similar trajectory, from the realm of matter to the realm of ideas?

What is ironic about the debate over the patenting of business methods and other intangible inventions is that it is nowhere more heated than on the Internet, itself a nonphysical and intangible realm in which "virtual" businesses composed of little more than hope and electrons are nonetheless creating very real and substantial wealth in the form of new products, new services, new jobs, and new economic growth for society. We find it odd that those who have no problem accepting the Net as the intangible fruit of nonphysical electronic innovation should get stuck in industrial-age conceptions of what should and should not be patentable.

> **Business-method patents are a fact of life today that no company can safely ignore.**

Odd perhaps, but not surprising. The expansion of patentable subject matter into new and ever more abstract realms has always met with resistance. Software patents were sharply condemned 10 years ago (and still are in some circles), as were biotechnology patents 20 years ago, and even patents involving telephony or other processes 130 years ago. In each case, critics warned that these new kinds of patents would be harmful to scientific discovery and innovation. And yet in each case, innovation and discovery actually intensified.

It seems reasonable, then, to suppose that the patenting of technology-enabled business ideas will likewise not inhibit innovation. But if it turns out that this latest expansion of patent rights proves to be socially or economically harmful, the courts will doubtless intervene, as they have in previous patent controversies. It will probably require three to five years of legal interpretation and policy debate before the scope and limits of business-method patents are clearly delineated.

One thing, however, is already clear. Whatever changes may occur in patent law tomorrow, business-method patents are an inarguable fact of life *today* that no company can safely ignore. We explore the implications of these new methods patents for e-commerce strategy in Chapter 7.

Patents Aren't Just for Big Companies Anymore

Many critics of the intellectual property system also contend that patents have become bludgeons used by large corporations to intimidate their smaller and more innovative competitors. This charge is bandied about so often these days that it is very nearly accepted as gospel. The facts, however, suggest otherwise. For example, the proportion of patent recipients who are first-time patentees (small start-up firms and independent inventors for the most part) has actually been rising dramatically for more than two decades now. In 1972, barely 5 percent of patents went to start-ups and other first-time patentees. By 1992, the number had skyrocketed to 23 percent of patent recipients.[21] In addition, research shows that although small firms spend only 3 percent of the amount that large corporations devote to research and development (R&D), they produce 15 percent of all patented innovations. It is no surprise that this dramatic surge in patenting by small companies corresponds precisely with the birth and development of the venture capital industry and the entrepreneurial high-tech sector of Silicon Valley.

To be sure, simply owning a patent does not necessarily mean that a small start-up has the economic wherewithal to assert that patent against large corporate infringers. But for every case in which a corporate behemoth uses its patents to bludgeon small competitors—more often they use their vast patent portfolios against each other—you can also find a case in which patents have been the only thing standing between a small start-up and its destruction at the hands of a vastly more powerful and richer Fortune 500 competitor. Take Stac Electronics's $120 million patent victory against Microsoft in 1996, for example, or tiny Fonar's $128.7 million verdict in 1997 against General Electric, the largest company on earth in terms of market capitalization. With the recent creation of both a "contingent patent bar" (i.e., patent lawyers who work on contingency) and affordable patent insurance that covers litigation costs, small companies will have an even better chance of asserting their rights against big firms.

The Problem of Internet Trash Patents

Not all the concerns surrounding today's patenting craze are imagined or overblown, however. One very real and serious problem is the growing rash of trash patents—that is, patents that don't really cover unique new inventions but, having been granted by overworked and underexperienced Patent and Trademark Office examiners anyway, are now being used by get-rich-quick Internet carpetbaggers to intimidate competitors or extort money from businesses fearful of the exorbitant costs of defending against a patent suit.

One of the most vocal critics of trash patents is Gregory Aharonian, editor of the *Internet Patent News Service*. "The PTO will issue 40,000 software patents in 1998 and 1999—10 times as many software patents as it [issued] six years ago," says Aharonian. "Since there is no way [the] agency can increase its output ten-fold while increasing its resources much less so, the quality of patents has dropped substantially."[22] According to Aharonian's research, more than 50 percent of these software patents cite *no* nonpatent prior art—that is, there are no references from engineering journals or other published nonpatent sources that describe previous work in the field. Argues Aharonian, "This means these patents should be presumed to be invalid."[23]

Prior art is indeed a critical issue in patent validity, for it is the only means of showing that the technology the applicant seeks to patent is truly novel and represents an advance over previous work in the field. Obviously, someone seeking to patent a flying saucer might not need to cite prior art in the technology because there probably isn't any. But for a software firm to try to patent some new database software, for example, without citing any of the 40 years of published research in this area is simply ludicrous. It is the statutory duty of patent applicants to disclose all relevant prior art in the technology of which they are aware, and then show why his or her innovation represents a genuinely new and nonobvious advance in that technology. Only then should a patent be granted.

Defeating Internet "Kitchen Sink" Patents

Insufficient prior art is not the only problem plaguing Internet patenting today. Some patents also assert wildly overbroad claims. We call these "kitchen sink" patents because they sometimes appear to be asserting ownership of everything under the sun, as many believe is the case with a patent owned by Sightsound that claims exclusive rights to *all* downloading of music or video over the Internet.

Then there are patents that claim ownership over technologies that were not even envisaged at the time the patent was originally applied for, as in the case of a patent for an application of videotext technology (now a defunct medium) that Wang claimed was infringed by Netscape's Internet browser (see Chapter 7). Another case involves a firm called E-Data, which employed a kitchen-sink claims expansion when it filed infringement suits against a dozen Internet firms. E-Data claimed these firms violated a patent, issued six years before the Web was even created, that supposedly covered *any* form of Web commerce in which software, music, or other products are downloaded directly into a user's computer. As with the Wang patent, the courts denied E-Data's claim, calling the suit "an obvious attempt to expand the scope of its patent beyond that which was intended." [24]

Strengthening the PTO as a National Resource

While the courts have invalidated all kitchen-sink and trash patents that have been challenged to date, the continuing proliferation of these improperly issued patents is worrisome. As was the case during the gold-rush phase of previous new economic frontiers, it seems that scam artists and claim jumpers are again trying to cash in without doing any of the real market-digging work of genuine entrepreneurs. One hundred and fifty years ago, such people used bogus land claims; today they use bogus patent claims.

Which is why, of course, a properly functioning "claims

office" is so important. Unfortunately, the PTO suffers from serious deficiencies in staffing, resources, and examination procedures that hamper its ability to conduct the sort of due diligence in patent applications that is required today. Clearly, something must be done about this problem if we want to ensure the integrity of the intellectual property system in the United States. The PTO is expanding its staff of examiners by 40 percent, from 2,500 to 3,500, and has announced plans to install new systems and databases for researching prior art. But much more needs to be done. PTO salaries must be raised significantly if the agency hopes to attract qualified computer scientists and software engineers as examiners. Employee incentives should also be shifted so that examiners are rewarded not for the number of applications processed, as is now the case, but for the quality of their examinations.

We suspect that, just as with previous crises in PTO history, the agency will eventually get its house in order. Too much of the economy—both our own and the world's—depends on a properly functioning system of intellectual property rights for the PTO to do otherwise. In a time when intellectual property is becoming the currency of the global economy, strengthening the PTO should be a national priority—and funded accordingly. In the meantime, we offer in Chapter 7 a few modest proposals that may at least eliminate the problem of trash patents.

Do Patents Help or Hinder Innovation?

In the end, however, the debate over patents boils down to one fundamental question: do they help or hinder innovation? Addressing precisely this issue in his 1999 book *Owning the Future,* author Seth Shulman argues that in a postindustrial economy such as ours, granting patent rights to vital knowledge assets will inevitably stifle innovation and foster monopolies that hoard scientific and medical discoveries to the detriment of society. Unless society limits these intellectual property rights, Shulman insists, we face "nothing less than an uncontrolled stampede to auction off our technological and cultural heritage . . . and the specter of an ominous descent into a new Dark Age." [25]

"A new Dark Age?" That's pretty scary stuff. The only problem, as *Business Week* magazine pointed out in its review of Shulman's book, "is that there's almost no evidence to support this bleak forecast." In fact, Shulman rather brazenly ignores key evidence that strongly contradicts his doomsday argument, making him, in the words of *Business Week,* "a less than fully trustworthy guide to a vexing and complicated area of the law." [26]

Shulman's frequent misrepresentations are indeed troubling. Consider, for example, his reportage of the five-year-long patent infringement suit against the biotechnology firm Cellpro. According to Shulman, innovative little Cellpro "developed a therapy" to treat a deadly type of lymphoma, but thanks to the greed of the pharmaceutical giant Baxter International, "Cellpro [was prevented] from offering its lifesaving treatment to dying patients." [27]

If true, the Cellpro case would certainly seem to be a horrific example of monopoly greed run amok. But the truth is more complex than what Shulman's reportage would have us believe. The stem-cell separation technique at issue was not "developed" by Cellpro at all; it was actually invented by Dr. Curt Civin at Johns Hopkins University in the 1980s and licensed first to Becton Dickinson in 1984 and then to Baxter International in 1990. All Cellpro did, as reported in the prestigious *National Law Journal,* was willfully purloin the technology and then use it to develop an experimental bone marrow treatment. Baxter claims

Cellpro then rebuffed its attempts to negotiate a licensing deal for the use of the technology.

In the bitter court battle that ensued, neither company could be said to have emerged unstained by charges of greed and neglect for the welfare of dying patients. But Cellpro's behavior was apparently so predatory that on July 24, 1997, U.S. District Judge Roderick R. McKelvie took the extraordinary steps of citing the company for "contempt for the law and for our system of civil justice" and then trebling the jury's infringement award against Cellpro to $6.9 million.[28] In his harshly worded 27-page opinion, the judge pointed out that Cellpro's attempt to portray itself as a "warrior in a twentieth-century holy crusade . . . is a facade constructed by the venture capitalists [whose] primary motivation is not humanitarianism nor even responsible capitalism." He also slapped the venture capitalists who first funded Cellpro, pointing out that they knew the company intended to infringe Baxter's patents and had even set aside $3 million to wage a legal defense against the patent suit that would inevitably result.[29]

It would appear that the heroes and villains in today's intellectual property wars are not always easily identified. In any event, Shulman's main argument—that patents harm society by stifling innovation and restricting the free flow and sharing of knowledge—deserves to be considered on its merits.

The Evidence for Patents' Economic Benefits

But even here Shulman seems disingenuous when he claims that "expert analysis of the broad economic effects of the intellectual property system is murky."[30] Because thanks to a vast storehouse of patent information going back many decades, the truth is that the patent system's effects on innovation activity and economic growth is actually one of the most richly studied subjects in the field of economics. Hundreds of academic studies on this issue are available to the public either for free or at nominal cost from the National Bureau of Economic Research,[31] and it is unfortunate that Shulman cites none in his book. For with surprising unanimity, nearly all these studies suggest that strong patent protection may actually be one of the most effective means of promoting innovation, knowledge sharing, and economic growth yet devised.

This conclusion may seem counterintuitive at first—after all, don't patents give their owners the right to exclude others from using a technology? Yes they do. But that is very different from denying to others the *knowledge* of the new technology itself, which patents by law are required to disclose in sufficient detail such that anyone "skilled in the arts" could replicate it. Moreover, all evidence indicates that when you deny others the right to copy your technology, you force them to innovate by designing around and improving upon your patent with more advanced discoveries of their own.

To explain how patent rights promote innovation and knowledge sharing, Professors Naomi Lamoreaux and Kenneth Sokoloff of the University of California at Los Angeles propose an interesting thought experiment in their study of late nineteenth- and early twentieth-century inventors:

> *Imagine a world in which there was no patent system to guarantee inventors property rights to their discoveries. In such a world, inventors would have every incentive to be secretive and to guard jealously their discoveries from competitors [because those discoveries] could, of course, be copied with impunity. By contrast, in a world where property rights in invention were protected, the situation would be very different. Inventors would now feel free to promote their discoveries as widely as possible so as to maximize*

returns either from commercializing their ideas themselves or from assigning rights to the idea to others. Competitors would have an incentive to keep tabs on what their rivals were doing [because] they could not risk investing in an invention without finding out how their discovery related to (and whether it replicated) technological developments in other sectors of the economy. The protections offered by the patent system would thus be an important stimulus to the exchange of technological information in and of themselves. Moreover, it is likely that the cross-fertilization that resulted from these information flows would itself be a potent stimulus to technological change.[32]

One needn't rely solely on thought experiments to conclude that the patent system does, in fact, work effectively to promote innovation and knowledge sharing. There is also plenty of research evidence to confirm that view. Professors Adam B. Jaffe of Brandeis University and Josh Lerner of Harvard Business School, for example, report that "the empirical and case study analyses suggest that the policy reforms of the 1980s had a dramatic and positive effect on technology commercialization."[33] These reforms strengthened patent rights and for the first time allowed federally funded research institutions to privately patent and license the fruits of their research.

Patents will be key in determining winners and losers in business competition.

The benefits of IP protection also extend far beyond the borders of the United States. According to Professor Jonathan Eaton of Boston University and Samuel Kortum, a member of the Board of Governors of the Federal Reserve, "international trade in ideas is a major factor in world growth . . . [and] all countries tap a common pool of knowledge, with a country's relative productivity depending on its ability to absorb that knowledge into its domestic technology."[34]

What is the most important determinant of a country's ability to tap that common pool of knowledge? Robert J. Barro, an economist with the Bank of England, and Spanish economics professor Xavier Sala-I-Martin conclude that it is not capital resources but rather the strength of a country's intellectual property protection (along with its education and infrastructure) that is the primary spur to technology diffusion and economic growth. Without strong intellectual property rights, they found, "the leading [countries] tend to have insufficient incentive to invent and the follower [countries] tend to have excessive incentive to copy" rather than invent for themselves.[35]

We could cite dozens of other studies by economists that also find the patent system to be, on balance, an effective instrument for fostering innovation and technology diffusion. We might also point to the extraordinary vitality of the U.S. economy itself as at least suggestive of the patent system's positive effect on innovation and economic growth.

But for all practical purposes, none of that really matters, does it? The reality is that patents exist, they are becoming increasingly important in determining the winners and losers of business competition, and every CEO in America simply has to deal with that fact.

We certainly don't mean to suggest that the patent system is without flaws, some of them (such as the trash patents problem) potentially serious enough to undermine the system itself. Nor do we wish to imply that the public policy questions regarding patents are anything but crucial for society to answer. What social and environmental costs, for example, may result from patenting sterile "terminator" seeds and other genetically engineered agricultural products? Should limits be imposed on corporate efforts to grab patent control over developing nations' native plants, a practice known as "bio-piracy"? How should universities deal with conflicts of interest between free and open academic research and the desire to profit from that research? And aren't some fundamental discoveries—the human genome, for example—so vital to the well-being of society that they ought to be placed in the public domain? We leave these vexing questions to other, more qualified writers.

HOW TO READ THIS BOOK

We have designed this book to be both a strategic and a practical guide to the real-world role and uses of patents in business competition today. Although we use the terms *patents* and *intellectual property* interchangeably throughout the book, patents are actually only one of several types of intellectual property—the legally protected form of intellectual assets—along with trade secrets, trademarks, and copyrights. We focus on patents for two reasons. First, patents are the most tangible form of intellectual property, they enjoy the strongest legal protection, and (except in the media and entertainment fields) they have the greatest impact on the commercial success and market value of firms today. Second, patent databases are a virtual Alexandrian Library of information that, when combined with new automated data-mining and visualization tools, make them potent competitive intelligence tools that businesses can use to great advantage.

Patents as Assets and Business Tools

In the chapters that follow, we show how companies can tap their patent portfolios for the hidden asset values and revenue streams that lie within. We present case studies of companies that have deployed their patents as competitive weapons to capture and defend markets, outflank and outmarket rivals, increase R&D

effectiveness, and achieve greater results in mergers, acquisitions, and joint venture activities. And we offer insights into how firms can mine the information contained in patents—the greatest source of competitive intelligence on earth—to map technology trends and convergences, uncover the strategies and capabilities of friend and foe alike, and strengthen the efforts of every functional unit in the enterprise, from R&D and marketing to finance, human resources, and mergers and acquisitions.

In discussing how companies can tap the asset values in intellectual property to achieve board and shareholder objectives, we pay particular attention to the use of patents to

- Generate new revenues through licensing

- Boost earnings per share and total shareholder return

- Improve return on investment for R&D and seed continuing innovation

- Raise corporate valuations and enhance equity and other financing opportunities

- Serve as the currency of mergers, acquisitions, and joint ventures

And in exploring the many ways that IP portfolios can serve as competitive tools, we show how senior executives and first-line managers can utilize patents to

- Plot competitors' product strategies, as well as ways to "patent-block" them

- Gain patent-protected entry into lucrative but hotly contested markets

- Acquire exclusive rights to emerging market-leading technologies

- Increase R&D effectiveness and avoid infringement minefields

- Detect possible infringers, as well as likely sources of licensing income

A Road Map to the Chapters

In the hope that this book will not only be read but *used,* we have organized it as follows. In Chapter 2, we explore the historic evolution of corporate policy and practice regarding intellectual property, showing how the lost art of using patents for competitive advantage is being rediscovered today at some of the world's leading firms. The economic drivers of this IP revitalization movement are traced, as are the reasons why patents have become so important in shaping competitive outcomes and enhancing the commercial success of enterprises.

Chapter 3 is aimed particularly at chief executives. In it we show how intellectual property strategy can significantly augment the CEO's efforts to build, prune, and sustain a high-growth business or portfolio of businesses—we call it the "Grow-Fix-Sell triage"—by boosting the effectiveness of R&D, finance, and business development, and opening up new strategy options for every business unit in the enterprise. We also outline some of the key organizational and leadership requirements necessary for the development and implementation of effective patent strategies. This patent-enhanced Grow-Fix-Sell triage provides the strategy framework for the remaining chapters of the book.

We then move to Chapter 4 for a discussion of the biggest long-term challenge, largest expense, and greatest risk for many companies: R&D. Large corporate R&D projects are often bet-the-company affairs, and, as you will read, some companies have unfortunately lost that bet and suffered catastrophic financial and market losses as a result of their failure to avoid the patent-infringement minefields that litter the landscape of business today. Besides addressing the risks of inadequate patent planning in R&D, the chapter also outlines the three building blocks of effective patent strategy—we call it *IP-3 for R&D*—that R&D managers must embrace if they wish to successfully navigate the landscape of competition, establish proprietary market positions, block competitors, and reinforce their product marketing and branding efforts.

Chapter 5 is about financial leverage. How can CFOs tap the value of that 75 percent of all corporate wealth today that consists of intangible knowledge assets? In this chapter, we show how CFOs can maximize the value of their underutilized patent assets to generate new revenue streams, reduce costs, and increase shareholder return. We also highlight some of the new ways that patents can become the "Rembrandts in the attic" that enhance a company's financing efforts and bolster its market valuation.

In Chapter 6, we explain how business development executives can use patent-driven merger and acquisition strategies to seize the technology high ground during major market shifts, gain patent-protected entry into lucrative new markets, and value and structure deals to maximum advantage. We also show how "patent mapping" can help companies (as well as IP-savvy investors) uncover the most profitable M&A opportunities of tomorrow.

Finally, Chapter 7 explores the unprecedented new power and reach that e-commerce patents now have to shape the competitive dynamics of today's explosive Internet industries. In e-commerce, the stakes are higher, the risks greater, and the impact of patents far more significant than with any previous industrial emergence in history. And with the Open Source movement playing a wildcard role in Net software development and business strategy, a finely tuned patent strategy could well mean the difference between success and failure.

A Final Caveat

We wish to stress that *Rembrandts in the Attic* is meant to serve only as a broad overview, a primer, on how companies can develop patent strategies that enhance their commercial success and create new shareholder wealth. While intellectual property management is indeed becoming a new core competency of successful enterprises, it is still only an embryonic field of corporate strategy development. More experience will yield deeper insights.

And we have one final caveat: this book is no substitute for professional legal counsel where needed. The authors have written a book about business strategy, not the law.

2

RESTORING THE
LOST ART OF PATENT STRATEGY

Outside it was hot enough to make even a Texas politician wilt. But inside the ballroom of the Four Seasons hotel in Austin on that sweltering July day in 1997, the mood was buoyant. It was the annual shareholders' meeting of the Dell Computer Corporation, and people were flush with excitement and anticipation as they waited for the company's brash young founder and CEO, college dropout-turned-billionaire Michael Dell, to deliver his keynote address.

Finally, a hush fell over the room. . . . Michael Dell had arrived. He made his way to the dais and, looking out over the audience, stood silently as the giant image of a chart was flashed up on the screen behind him. The chart compared Dell's stock performance over the past three years to six other big-time stock market winners—

Microsoft, Gillette, Coca-Cola, Intel, Cisco Systems, and rival PC-maker Compaq Computer—and it showed that Dell's stock had soared upward at twice the rate of the stocks of the other companies. The audience gasped.

Dell stood there, savoring the reaction. Then, grinning, he finally spoke: "And that concludes our presentation." There was a moment of stunned silence, and then the crowd erupted. According to a reporter who witnessed the event, "The applause [was] deafening."[1]

Two years later, shareholders have even more to celebrate. With 1999 revenues topping $18 billion and profits of nearly $1.5 billion, Dell is clearly the driving force in the PC business, even challenging industry kingpin Compaq Computer for top ranking in global PC market share. It is the largest computer merchant on the Internet, selling over $30 million worth of PCs on-line every day. And as for the company's stock, it just keeps rising, rising, rising. According to the *Wall Street Journal*, which named Dell its 1999 Best Performing Company, the PC maker has earned 223 percent in compound annual total return to shareholders in the last three years.

Ironically, the secret to Dell's high-tech success has little to do with technology itself—its PCs, though of good quality, are made with mostly off-the-shelf components. Nor are low prices the key to the company's stellar performance, for one can certainly find less expensive computers elsewhere. Rather, as *Business Week* noted when it named Dell No. 1 on its 1998 "InfoTech 100" list of the top technology companies in America, "Dell Computer has ridden the direct sales of PCs into the stratosphere [by] redefining customer service."[2]

Actually, Dell's real accomplishment was to transform a commodity "white-box" business into a brand-name gold mine with margins that make its competitors weep. It has done this by pioneering a unique "build-to-order" direct sales model that enables buyers to order a custom-configured PC via the Internet or an 800 number. These orders are then processed through a continuous-flow manufacturing, configuration, and customer service operation for delivery to home or office within 72 hours. For PC shoppers, most of whom would rather stick needles in their eyes than endure the slacker-style indifference of retail stores, Dell's "have it your way" PCs and top-notch 24-hour service and support are a godsend. For Dell, this build-to-order system has resulted in the highest margins and the lowest manufacturing and inventory costs in the industry, a cash- conversion cycle (the difference between the time it pays its creditors and the time it takes to get paid) of an incredible *negative* eight days, and the fervent loyalty (not to mention the repeat business) of millions of satisfied customers.

It has also earned Dell the unabashed envy of its competitors, several of whom are now attempting to mimic its direct sales approach. When archrival Compaq unveiled its own build-to-order effort in late 1998, for example, one dealer explained it this way: "They are going for the Dell model. You can't really blame them. They have been getting beat up by Dell."[3]

Imitation, of course, is the highest form of flattery. But as Dell's director of intellectual property and assistant general counsel, Henry Garrana, is quick to point out, "Imitation is also the easiest infringement case to make."

Infringement? Yes. As in patent infringement. For unbeknownst to its rivals, Dell has already secured 4 patents on its build-to-order direct sales model. And by the time you read this book, an additional 38 patents still pending on this system may also have been granted. These patents cover not only the on-line customer-configurable ordering system, but also the way it is integrated into the company's manufacturing, inventory, distribution, and customer service operations. In short, Dell has patented its pioneering method of doing business.

"It may sound easy to produce and sell millions of PCs, where each one is custom configured by the customer, but it is not a simple task," notes Garrana. "This is our innovation—how we run the factory, how our ordering system allows customers to configure their PCs with whatever hardware and software they choose, how we advise customers of shipment—and we intend to protect that innovation."

This is a rather unorthodox intellectual property strategy, to be sure, especially for a firm competing in a commodity business like computers. Most companies, to the extent that they even have patent strategies, focus those strategies on protecting their products or technologies. Dell, however, uses its patents to protect and leverage the most valuable component of its business and the true source of its competitive advantage: its build-to-order business model.

To Garrana, this approach makes perfect sense. "If you want to have a successful IP program, you have to focus on the things that you do that bring real value to the market," he insists. "You cannot focus on anything else. That's why we try to patent those aspects of our business that add the most value and make us successful."

The question now is, What does Dell intend to do with its patents? In the spring of 1999, the company cross-licensed its patents to IBM in a $16 billion deal that enabled each to plug key holes in their respective businesses. Dell gained access to IBM's patented PC components, and IBM obtained access to Dell's patented systems for running a successful build-to-order direct sales effort.

But what will Dell do if other rivals such as Compaq try to copy its build-to-order direct sales systems too closely? "Our strategy to deal with infringers is confidential," is all Garrana will say.

THE ECLIPSE OF PATENTS

Dell's highly strategic approach to patenting is a relatively new phenomenon within corporate America. Until very recently, in fact, few CEOs ever used the words *patents* and *strategy* in the same sentence. Patents were seen merely as legal instruments, to be filed away in the corporate counsel's office and forgotten. Strategy, on the other hand, was that opaque and slippery stuff that the people in the executive suite were supposed to hammer into shape. What did one have to do with the other?

Oddly enough, the great-great-grandfathers of most of these CEOs would have found it easy to answer that question, for nineteenth-century businesses put a lot of stock in the power of patents to help them dominate markets and keep competitors at bay. In the "Great Telegraph Wars" of the 1870s, for example, financiers Cornelius Vanderbilt and Jay Gould hurled all manner of legal, financial, and competitive assaults at each other as they ruthlessly schemed to control the most valuable assets in the industry: Thomas Edison's telegraph patents. Both these men knew—and rightly so—that robber-baron-sized fortunes depended on those patents.

Fears of Antitrust Action

Beginning around the 1930s, however, the strategic value and uses of patents were largely lost to business. This was partly due to the U.S. government's antitrust policy, which in the 1930s began to treat patents as anticompetitive by their very nature. The Antitrust Division of the Justice Department and the Federal Trade Commission (FTC) both created special sections devoted exclusively to antipatent litigation. As a result, most companies learned to avoid doing anything with their patents that might attract these agencies' attentions because firms that were too aggressive in using patents to block competitors and maintain their margins quickly got into trouble. In 1975, for example, Xerox was forced to sign an FTC consent decree that required it to license its xerographic patents to friend and foe alike. As a result, a tsunami of lower-priced Japanese copiers flooded the U.S. market, and Xerox's market leadership was washed away. The consent decree also contributed in no small measure to Xerox's failure to patent many of the new computer technologies it developed in the late 1970s (see Chapter 3). To be sure, the company's own myopia regarding the market potential of these technologies didn't help matters any. But as long-time Xerox managers will tell you, after the consent decree Xerox was simply gun-shy about patenting *anything*.

For this and other reasons, patents came to be viewed not as profit-generating assets but rather as cost centers of dubious value. They were rarely employed as offensive business tools to gain market advantage—one exception being pharmaceutical firms, which relied on them to help build the most profitable industry in history. Instead, patents were for the most part regarded as *defensive* legal shields only, whose role was akin to that of the nuclear arsenals of the United States and Soviet Union during the cold war; that is, they were deterrents only, meant never (it was hoped) to be used.

It Was a Mad, Mad World

Under this MAD (mutual assured destruction) approach to intellectual property, patents served as bargaining chips, to be traded off or cross-licensed between firms as a means of forestalling costly patent infringement lawsuits that often benefited no one (except the lawyers). The thinking was, If you sue me, then I'll sue you back, and in the end we'll both just wind up with radioactive balance sheets.

The MAD strategy also governed international patent activity, at least in Japan. "The traditional corporate strategy in Japan has been to emphasize quantity over quality," explains Japanese patent commissioner Takeshi Isayama. "Patents were mostly to protect rather than to sell. At present, there are about 900,000 valid patents in Japan, and about 600,000 of them are not used as fully as they could be."[4]

This is not to say that businesses never used patent protection to stop competitors from copying their products or technologies. But filing a patent infringement lawsuit was, at least until fairly recently, an iffy proposition at best. For one thing, the trial and appellate courts that heard patent cases had geographical rather than subject-matter jurisdiction, which meant that they were not terribly savvy about the complexities of patent law. Moreover, there was wide variation in what each court considered to be a "valid" patent. In one district, the court never found a patent it considered valid—not in 50 years of rulings![5] The system was not entirely unpredictable, though: patent holders could be pretty sure they would lose. On average, the courts denied 75 percent of claims against alleged infringers.[6]

There were some exceptions, as noted earlier. Gil Amelio, former CEO at both National Semiconductor and Apple, contrasts the lackadaisical approach to patent issues in recent years to the "good old days" back at Bell Labs in the 1960s: "When I started work there in 1968, they put you through this orientation program that was totally focused on intellectual property. In fact, they even said something to the effect that here at Bell Labs, we don't make products, we make paper—meaning patents. And it's true. Our performance was measured on only two things: getting patents, and getting important papers published. We were also required to keep detailed patent notebooks of our work. I learned, by the way, just how smart they were about those notebooks when Northern Telecomm contested our patent on the CCD [the charged couple device of which Amelio himself was a key inventor] and claimed they invented it first. Well, it turned out that it was my patent notebook that won the case for Bell Labs, and that was a victory that was probably worth hundreds of millions of dollars to the company."

Missing the IP Boat in Silicon Valley

In any event, if most traditional enterprises tended to value their patents principally for their deterrent effect, the new high-tech companies that arose in the late 1970s in Silicon Valley tended to value them not at all. For one thing, software as an independent invention was not even considered patentable until court rulings in the late 1980s forced the Patent and Trademark Office (PTO) to revise its policies. But even after those rulings, most firms continued until recently to copyright their software rather than seek patent coverage.

Sometimes this was due to simple ignorance of the greater legal protections and business advantages that patents offer. "Absolutely, if we had known better we would have patented NetWare," concedes David Bradford, vice president and general counsel at networking software maker Novell, whose NetWare is used by 85 percent of Fortune 1000 firms. "If you have a patented technology that becomes a standard, then the licensing fees you derive can be enormous."

Other companies opposed software patenting for reasons of competitive self-interest, although this view was often couched in statesmanlike warnings that patenting would spark a frenzy of costly and destructive litigation. "[We] oppose the patentability of software," declared database software giant Oracle Corporation in written testimony presented to PTO hearings on software patenting in 1994. "[Patents] are not appropriate for industries such as software development," the firm insisted, as these would "only drain capital resources which are better spent on software development." This testimony was somewhat suspect, however, given that Oracle had already begun patenting its own software (albeit only "defensively," the company claimed). But the real motivation for Oracle's opposition to software patenting may actually have stemmed from growing concerns that Microsoft was, as *Forbes* later reported, "aggressively encircling its database competitor [with patents], presaging future troubles for Oracle."[7] Or perhaps, as some insiders suggest, Oracle CEO Larry Ellison was simply worried that a very powerful company—say, IBM?— might somehow get the notion that a portion of its patented, legally protected technology had mysteriously made its way into Oracle software.

Still another important reason for Silicon Valley's early antipathy toward patents was the freewheeling "garage start-up" culture of the high-tech community itself. Many developers saw patents as nothing more than monopolistic clubs wielded by corporate behemoths to crush visionary innovators. Prominent Washington patent attorney Robert Greene Sterne remembers the reception he got in the mid-1980s when he lectured to Silicon Valley entrepreneurs about software patents. "I would get laughed out of the room," he recalls. "I'd get booed. I'd be called a capitalist pig by software entrepreneurs who thought it should be owned by the masses."[8]

Such anticapitalist sentiment survives even today, of course, especially among some in the Internet community who argue that "information wants to be free" (and you can be sure these people have never had to foot the cost of putting a content site up on the Web). A more sophisticated and nuanced view of patenting, however, is offered by the Open Source software movement. This loose-knit but highly influential grouping of independent developers and businesses calls not for an end to patenting per se (although they wouldn't shed any tears if the U.S. Patent and Trademark Office were to suddenly shut its doors) but rather for the granting of royalty-free licenses and other concessions that would allow free-software developers to continue doing the sort of collaborative work that has already contributed so much to making the Internet a robust communications and commercial medium. The challenges that the Open Source movement poses to companies seeking to develop effective patent strategies for the burgeoning e-commerce marketplace are explored in Chapter 7.

A Strictly Balance-Sheet Focus

Finally, the whole array of corporate culture and practices of the time tended to preclude a great deal of attention being paid to intellectual property or, indeed, any intangible assets. For one thing, until recently there wasn't a business school in the country that offered courses or seminars on intellectual property—and you'd still be hard-pressed to find one today. Then, too, we didn't see "knowledge" companies such as Microsoft attracting market capitalizations 32 times greater than their book values (or, for that matter, 7 times more than that of an industrial firm such as General Motors, which has 10 times the revenues of Microsoft). Nor did we have Internet companies with price-to-book ratios of . . . actually, how do you compute the ratio when the book value is a negative number? No, in those days a corporate balance sheet actually meant something, and a chief executive could depend on it to provide at least a reasonably accurate picture of his (and in those days, it surely was *his*) company's exploitable asset base.

In sum, then, for most of this century intellectual property played only a minimal role in shaping the commercial and strategic fortunes of American business. Patents were for the most part used defensively, if at all, and few companies outside the pharmaceutical, biotechnology, or certain other sectors ever thought of them as strategic assets. As for America's chief executives, suffice it to say that few if any had even heard of such a thing as a "VP of Intellectual Property," let alone hired one.

A NEW ALCHEMY OF WEALTH

But then a funny thing happened on the way to the millennium. Actually, a whole series of changes occurred—legal, technological, and most of all economic—that together created a new alchemy of corporate wealth creation in which intellectual property has come to play a powerful new role as a strategic asset and competitive weapon of enormous value.

In 1982, a new specialized Court of Appeals of the Federal Circuit (CAFC) was created by act of Congress, with a 12-judge panel deeply schooled in patent law. This new circuit court not only brought a much-needed uniformity to patent doctrine and led to greater consistency in lower district court trial rulings, but also set new precedents that enhanced the rights of patent holders and the efficacy of patents themselves. Since the creation of the CAFC, the trend in patent rulings has been exactly opposite of that which had prevailed previously. Whereas prior to the CAFC, 75 percent of patent claims were denied, today about 75 percent are upheld, with substantially larger damage awards being levied against infringers than previously.

The creation of the CAFC wasn't the only legal change during the 1980s that enhanced the value and power of patents. The passage of the Bayh-Dole Act permitted federal agencies for the first time to grant patent rights to nonprofit and federally funded research centers. In addition, the U.S. Supreme Court reversed its previous stance that held patents to be inherently anticompetitive and instead endorsed strong intellectual property rights as vital in fostering innovation. Combined with the relaxation of federal antitrust laws related to corporate joint ventures in R&D, these shifts in the legal landscape of the 1980s had the effect of enhancing the power of patents.

As a result, businesses began to discover (or, more accurately, rediscover) that patents could be important to their competitive goals. One recent study of patenting trends reported that in technology-intensive industries such as semiconductors and computers, where the legal rights to technologies are distributed across a diverse array of firms, the last 15 years saw a great increase in companies' use of patents as "bargaining chips in negotiations with other [companies], in gaining access to needed technologies, or in safeguarding against threats of costly litigation."[9] This has been especially true for the bigger firms with large sunk costs in manufacturing facilities and a need to draw on product or process technologies for which the patents were held by an array of companies.

Intellectual property has become a strategic asset and competitive weapon of enormous value.

Smaller firms have found their own strategic uses for patents during the last 15 years as well. The same study cited earlier noted that smaller semiconductor design firms have found patents valuable in "attracting venture capital funds and securing proprietary rights in niche product markets."[10] And in the biotech sector, another study reported that the growing use of patents has "encouraged" smaller firms to patent aggressively in previously unexplored niche areas in order to "avoid the shadows of larger competitors."[11] Thus, even when employed for competitive purposes, patents appear to have also had the effect (perhaps ironically) of fostering innovation in new areas of research as well.

Learning Patent Lessons the Hard Way

Each of today's IP-savvy companies has its own particular story of awakening. In Microsoft's case, two incidents in the early 1990s were critical in shaking the software giant loose from its previous lethargy regarding patents and transforming it into one of the most aggressive IP practitioners in America. The first, say insiders, involved a threat by Digital Equipment Corporation (DEC, since acquired by Compaq) to sue Microsoft for patent infringement after a former top developer at DEC, David Cutler, went to work for Microsoft and reportedly employed certain of DEC's software innovations in the development of Windows NT. Microsoft ended up paying DEC $160 million to drop the matter—the two companies termed it a "strategic marketing agreement." Microsoft learned a second painful lesson when, under threat of an IBM patent suit, it agreed to pay $30 million to license certain of Big Blue's patents. In addition, IBM required Microsoft to provide it with Windows 3.1 code through September 1993, which IBM used to ensure the compatibility of its competing operating system, OS/2, with Windows. Having to license its Windows code—its principal competitive advantage— was especially onerous to Microsoft.

In a memo to key Microsoft employees around the time of these incidents, Bill Gates noted that the solution to the firm's growing patent problems was "patenting as much as we can."[12]

And that's exactly what Microsoft has done: assembled a power-ful patent portfolio so that it can never be "held up" by others' patent claims again. The sources of other companies' patent awakenings were different. Dell, for example, began assembling patents in the early 1990s only after being sued for contributory infringement because some of its vendors' components infringed on a third party's patents. Under U.S. patent law, that made Dell an infringer as well. In addition, Dell faced mounting patent licensing costs for its components as its business grew. As a result, Dell's IP strategy shifted from a defensive one aimed at prevent-ing infringement losses to an offensive one aimed at strengthen-ing and leveraging its build-to-order competitive advantage. For other companies, the stimulus was simply hearing about the famous Polaroid infringement suit against Kodak, which resulted in a $1 billion damage order in 1986 and forced the complete dismantling of Kodak's entire instant photography business (see Chapter 4). The case had a powerful impact on the thinking of executives throughout corporate America.

Whatever the catalyst in each case, though, the net result is that the landscape of patent activity in corporate America has changed dramatically since the formation of the CAFC 18 years ago. The number of new patents issued each year has nearly tripled, from the 40,000 to 60,000 per year that had prevailed during most of this century until the mid-1980s, to about 155,000 today. Not only has the total number of new patents soared, but the *rate of growth* in patenting is likewise on the rise, especially in software, communications, and other fast-paced technology sectors.

A Plethora of Lawsuits

Perhaps to no one's surprise, this explosion in patenting has also sparked a corollary boom in patent litigation. In the last ten

years, the number of patent suits filed each year has nearly doubled.[13] Observed the *New York Times,* "The 12-gauge lawsuit
[now holds] a prominent place in the corporate gun cabinet."
The paper attributed the proliferation of "strategic suing" to the
"combination of more patents and more companies built around
patented technology."[14]

Adds patent attorney John Lynch, "What's happening is that
more people are suing because patents are more valuable."[15]
Many bemoan this trend, including the chief executive of a firm
that is a defendant in a patent suit, who blames it on the fact that
some people simply have too much "patent testosterone" in their
blood. His company, he insists, prefers to "win in the marketplace, not the courtroom."[16] But there's another side to this issue.
Should anyone be allowed to "win in the marketplace" by illegally
taking for his or her own use—without payment or permis-
sion—the hard-earned fruits of another's costly investment of
time, money, and ingenuity? Of course not; that's why patent
laws and the courts exist.

In any event, it's important to keep this litigious trend in
perspective. The 2,120 patent suits filed in 1998 represent barely
1 percent of new patents issued that year,
and less than one-tenth of 1 percent of
the roughly 2.5 million total active patents. What's more, while the number of
suits filed has jumped, the number that
go to trial has remained stable over the
past decade at a little over 100 per year.

Like it or not, smart companies will develop strategies to deal with the threat of patent suits.

In point of fact, today's patent litiga-
tion rate is far lower than it was 100 years ago during the industrial revolution's great patenting upsurge. Alexander Graham Bell
alone, for example, fought over 600 separate patent infringement
suits in the 1880s, and in those days such suits were almost a
form of popular theater, as closely watched by the public as was
the more recent O.J. Simpson trial or Bill Clinton's impeachment

hearings. During one of Bell's patent trials in 1883, his firm's stock price plunged 50 points in just one day after shareholders following the daily testimony concluded (erroneously) that Bell might lose.[17] Be that as it may, when one includes all patent suits filed by *all* companies during that decade, today's so-called litigious society begins to look positively civilized.

Nevertheless, there is no denying that some companies today use patent suits—or simply the *threat* of patent suits—as key elements of their business strategies. Barr Laboratories, for example, has earned $200 million in recent years by challenging patents it considers "breakable" in court and forcing their owners to either supply their patented drugs to Barr for generic sale (such as Zeneca Group's Tamoxifen) or else pay annual fees to make Barr go away (such as the $30 million a year Bayer will pay until the year 2003). Its biggest case ever, a challenge to Lilly's Prozac patents, was settled in January 1999, when Lilly paid Barr $4 million to go away—a cheap price compared with the $1 billion in yearly revenue Lilly would have lost had Barr broken those Prozac patents. As Barr's CEO Bruce L. Downey, who is himself a former patent attorney, conceded, "A component of our business is to set about looking for [breakable patents]."

Whatever the merits or morality of Barr's litigationist business strategy, it is clear that patent suits have become potent competitive weapons today. One need not be either pro- or anti-litigation to recognize that in the real world of business, smart companies will develop both offensive and defensive strategies for dealing with this threat.

FRIENDLY COURTS OR TECH BOOM?

The debate over strategic suing only begs the larger question, however: Is the recent explosion in patenting activity—and the corresponding boom in patent litigation—merely the byproduct of the more patent-friendly legal environment created by the CAFC? This is a question of supreme importance, for it challenges the notion that intellectual property has any genuine value or utility for business—other than as a license to sue, that is. Have patents become just another corporate crack in the pavement, as it were, that the unscrupulous will pretend to trip over in order to achieve their nefarious get-rich-quick aims?

As it turns out, this "friendly court" hypothesis has already been tested and been found wanting. In their landmark 1997 study "Stronger Protection or Technological Revolution: What's Behind the Recent Surge in Patenting?" Boston University economics professor Samuel Kortum and Harvard Business School economist Joshua Lerner examined U.S. and international patent statistics along a number of parameters. They discovered that "contrary to the suggestion of the friendly court hypothesis . . . it appears that the jump in patenting reflects an increase in U.S. innovation." Moreover, noted the researchers, "the increase in patenting appears to be uniformly distributed [among both large firms and small start-ups], with the relative share of patents by new and small patentees actually increasing more dramatically than in the past."[18]

This last point is especially significant. The fact that the share of patents received by first-time patentees has more than quadrupled—from 5 percent a decade before the CAFC was formed to 23 percent a decade after its formation—suggests that a grassroots technological revolution of extraordinary scale and intensity is indeed underway throughout the world.

Could there really have been any doubt? Indeed, anyone with eyes to see cannot help but be awed by the whirlwind of artistic, scientific, and technological innovation that is now sweeping across the length and breadth of the globe. Indeed, humanity's march of progress has become a full-speed sprint into the next millennium, with new products and services and cultural works of all types (and all qualities) issuing forth from every corner of the globe at an ever more rapid rate. We may blame these whipping winds of change for much of the dislocation, alienation, and confusion of values that now afflicts our societies. We may hope, or even confidently expect, that humanity will eventually find its bearings once again, just as we always have in the past after confronting traumatic change. But we cannot doubt that something really *big* is happening.

This technological revolution, moreover, has also become inextricably entwined in a feedback loop with a deepening economic transformation—each is both cause and continuing effect of the other—that has altered not only the nature of markets but the sources of wealth formation and competitive advantage as well. Markets have become globalized and more efficient, offering even Taliban warriors in the mountains of Afghanistan the chance to buy Tommy Hilfiger T-shirts on their way to the adulteress stoning. Meanwhile, just-in-time everything and ever more rapid product turns have spawned a truly 24/7 process of technology development. Marxists used to speak of "continuous revolution," but their version was nothing compared with the dizzying nonstop pace of innovation today. And this continuous innovation has thrust knowledge itself—especially that which is codified into legal rights and called *intellectual property*—to the very top of the economic value chain.

Why Innovation Has Value

To those who ask why, the simple answer is the one given by 1930s-era bank robber Willie Sutton when asked why he robbed banks: "Because that's where the money is." And sure enough, ideas really *are* where the money is. They are the most important factor of production, the key link in the value chain, the highest value-added component of any product or service. Fifteen thousand years ago, if you wanted to increase social wealth, you invented a better spear because with it you could deliver more mastadon meat to the communal campfire. Fifteen hundred years ago, the most potent seeds of wealth formation were agricultural surpluses. And one hundred fifty years ago, you were really sitting in the catbird seat of wealth creation if you owned an iron mine and some machines to forge it into usable steel. Today? Well, which would you rather own: an iron mine or a new mining technology? A steel mill or the Windows operating system that runs its computers?

"I see this coming out of a change in our economy from one that is industrial-based to one that is knowledge-based, where intellectual property, soft assets, and other intangibles increasingly make up the bulk of the asset base for wealth production in our society" explains former Securities and Exchange (SEC) commissioner Steven Wallman, now a senior fellow at the Brookings Institution.[19] Wallman spearheaded an SEC task force several years ago to study ways of reforming financial disclosure and accounting rules to better recognize intangible assets (a similar effort is now underway at the Financial Accounting Standards Board). Adds Wallman, "If you have an accounting model that is biased against a whole set of assets, the result is going to be less efficient allocation of resources." The lack of meaningful disclosure about the value of intellectual property also forces investors to discount the value of a firm's intangibles and understate its earnings projections (unless it's a Net stock, in which case nothing shakes investor hopes). This tends to lower share values and increase the cost of capital, which impedes growth.

As *Forbes* recently observed, "The old [accounting] system served well enough when most assets were physical: plants and equipment, ore or oil in the ground, real estate, trees, inventory you could count and money that people owed you. But today the best assets are intangible: Microsoft's know-how and market position, Dell's exclusive marketing setup."[20]

Even so, the values are hard to miss. A 1997 study by Coopers & Lybrand (since merged with Price Waterhouse) found that two-thirds of the then-$7 trillion market value of all publicly traded U.S. companies is not even shown on their balance sheets because it lies not in their real estate or plant and equipment but in their intangible assets such as intellectual property.[21] Charles Handy, a fellow at the London School of Business, figures that a firm's IP assets are usually worth three to four times the firm's tangible book value.[22] Yet despite the hidden nature of these assets, the market has somehow detected their value. Whereas the overall ratio of stock prices to book values stood at 1.6 or so for most of this century, in recent years it has soared to about 5.3, where it stands today.

In one sense, perhaps, the primacy of ideas over matter in driving wealth formation may be nothing new at all. Stanford University economist and professor Paul Romer, who the *Wall Street Journal* calls the "father of the knowledge economy," points out that when John D. Rockefeller pumped out a barrel of crude, it only become truly valuable when he figured out what to do with it. The same was true of McDonald's in the 1950s, says Romer. Its success was due not to the hamburgers but to Ray Krock's ingenious ideas about how to mass-produce them and systematize their sale through branded franchised outlets coast to coast.

"Perhaps what is really new and most important about the knowledge economy," suggests Romer, "is not the products—not the computers or the telecommunications or the new financial services—but the fact that the recipes for making these products, the ideas and intellectual property behind them, are achieving more prominence. What's really starting to get people's attention is that there are enormous values associated with the property rights to these ideas."

IP Offers the Greatest Strategic Advantage

Chief among the reasons for these enormous values is the fact that, in the words of economist Lester Thurow, "skills and knowledge have become the only source of sustainable long-term competitive advantage."[23]

As goods and factor markets have become more efficient and accessible, expanding to reach every corner of the globe, the domains in which competitive advantage can be built have correspondingly narrowed. After all, only that which is unique to you and not accessible to your competitors—for example, your knowledge, skills, and business methods—can offer ground upon which you can differentiate yourself in business. Cheaper shoes, more shoes, even selling those shoes 24 hours a day—none of these offers much of an advantage anymore because anyone else can do the same. But a better way to track shifting consumer tastes in shoes and then rapidly meet the demand with new styles? There's money in that idea.

Are Wal-Mart's sandals, for example, any better than those sold by Sears or Kmart? Doubtful. But the sophisticated software and other information technology underlying Wal-Mart's logistical and marketing operations most certainly are. And it is these intellectual assets that have become the key to Wal-Mart's competitive advantage because they enable the company to deliver more efficient and satisfactory service to its customers than can its competitors. Similarly, Dell Computer has hardly vaulted to the top of the PC

"Skills and knowledge have become the only source of sustainable competitive advantage."

business because its computers are necessarily any better than those of its rivals. In fact, the "product" that Dell is selling is not even computers per se, but rather a hassle-free way for customers to buy a reliable, custom-configured PC that will be delivered to their door and then backed up by top-notch 24-hour service and support. The skills, technologies, and business methods that make this build-to-order direct sales model possible are Dell's unique innovation and the real secret of its competitive advantage.

But notice the difference in how Wal-Mart and Dell leverage their respective competitive advantages. As we noted earlier, Dell has patented its fundamental methods of doing business—the ideas and technologies manifested in its continuous-flow manufacturing, sales, marketing, distribution, and service systems—precisely because they are its most valuable assets and the key source of its competitive advantage. Wal-Mart, on the other hand, did not patent-protect its information systems or innovative methods of doing business. Thus when key employees left to join the Internet companies Amazon.com and Drugstore.com in 1998, Wal-Mart was reduced to filing a trade secret lawsuit against the two firms to try to protect its competitive advantage. Trade secrets are notoriously ineffective as intellectual property tools, so it was hardly a surprise when Wal-Mart ultimately settled the suit in April 1999, winning nothing of significance except the face-saving reassignment of a couple of Amazon.com's employees.

How ironic that Wal-Mart, a company that doubtless goes to great lengths to protect its $13 sandals from shoplifters, would not similarly protect the competitive ace in the hole of its entire $138 billion a year retailing empire with patents. Even more ironic is the fact that the design for those $13 sandals actually *is* patented—but not by Wal-Mart, or so claimed a company called

Teva, which sued and won a settlement from Wal-Mart in 1998 for patent infringement!

THE CHALLENGE FOR EXECUTIVES

This, then, is the real challenge for management today. It's not enough to make or do things that you can sell. Nor is it necessarily even enough to make or do or sell things in innovative ways—Xerox before the arrival of new CEO Richard Thoman is certainly proof of that, as seen in the next chapter. It's *what you do* with that innovation—*how you manage and utilize your intellectual property assets* in conjunction with all the other assets of your company to grow, fix, or sell your business—that determines whether you win or lose.

As one scholarly management journal recently put it, "The competitive advantage of firms in today's economy stems not from market position, but from difficult to replicate knowledge assets and the manner in which they are

How you configure and deploy your IP assets may determine whether you win or lose.

deployed. How these competencies and knowledge assets are configured and deployed will dramatically shape competitive outcomes and the commercial success of the enterprise."[24]

How, indeed, is the subject of our next chapter.

3

THE NEW
CEO CHALLENGE

G. Richard Thoman is not your typical chief executive officer. Most Fortune 500 CEOs, when asked how they intend to increase shareholder value, will usually talk about sales growth or cost-cutting or mergers and acquisitions. But Thoman, the 54-year-old newly appointed CEO of the $20 billion Xerox Corporation, is not content with such conventional balance-sheet strategies. Instead—and it's surprising to hear this from a former chief financial officer for IBM—he believes that a critical key to Xerox's future lies in something so intangible, so invisible to traditional bottom-line thinking and corporate practice, that it doesn't even show up on the balance sheet.

"My focus is intellectual property," he declares. "I'm convinced that the management of intellectual property is how value-added is going to be created at Xerox. And not just here, either. Increasingly, companies that are good at managing IP will win. And ones that aren't will lose."

Intellectual property? These words aren't even in the vocabularies of many CEOs, let alone their business strategies. Indeed, most chief executives still regard patents and other intellectual property as legal rather than business matters that are best left to the corporate attorneys to fuss over while they concentrate on the truly strategic stuff of competitive warfare.

Not Rick Thoman. Where others see mere legal instruments, he sees business tools. And where others see obscure pieces of paper gathering dust in the corporate legal office, he sees Rembrandts in the attic just waiting to be exploited for profit and competitive advantage.

To understand why Thoman thinks this way, you have to go back to his days as CFO at IBM. There, he saw firsthand how an aggressive intellectual property effort boosted patent licensing royalties a phenomenal 3,300 percent, from $30 million in 1990 to $1 billion annually today. This $1 billion per year, it should be noted, is largely *free cash flow*. In other words, we're talking about $1 billion in net annual recurring revenues—one-ninth of IBM's yearly pretax profits—flowing straight to the bottom line. To match that sort of net revenue stream, IBM would probably have to sell $20 billion worth of additional products each year, or an amount equal to one-fourth its total worldwide sales.

Even the most uninspired of bean-counting CFOs would have to be mightily impressed with returns like these, and Rick Thoman is anything but uninspired. In fact, he intends to mine a lot more than just revenues from his company's rich portfolio of patents. Properly managed and deployed, he believes, those intellectual property assets could enable Xerox to finally overcome the competitive drift that has plagued the company for decades and help Xerox regain its proper leadership role in the global technology industry.

Truth be told, Xerox could use the help. Here, after all, is a company that has been one of the great innovators of the twentieth century—a company that transformed the modern office with such inventions as the first automatic copier machine in 1959, the first desktop fax machine in 1966, the original laser printer in 1977, and the first computer networking system, called Ethernet, in 1979. Yet here, too, is a company known for "fumbling the future"[1] (as the title of one book put it) by failing to patent or commercialize other ground-breaking inventions of the 1970s and 1980s such as the personal computer, the graphical user interface underlying today's Windows and Macintosh operating system software, and a host of other technologies.

"We're the only technology company widely believed to have wasted its technology, at least historically," Thoman concedes. And it wasn't just technology that was wasted. Because Xerox lost its intellectual property advantage—the "allowed monopoly" that patents grant their owners—it also saw its once-fat margins wither and the 40 to 45 percent annual growth rate it enjoyed in the 1960s shrivel to the single digits in the decades ever since.

Xerox took some steps toward reversing this technological decline in the early 1990s. The company stepped up its R&D efforts and in 1996 formed Xerox New Enterprises as a business development vehicle to spin off separate companies that could develop and bring to market promising new technologies that fell outside Xerox's core businesses. Two of these start-ups, Documentum and Document Sciences Corporation, are now publicly traded firms.

Nonetheless, even at the time of Thoman's hiring in 1997, Xerox was still a sleeping giant when it came to exploiting its intellectual property assets. It owned some 8,000 patents, yet no one in the company could say with any assurance precisely which, or how many, of these patents had any significant commercial or strategic value. Moreover, although Xerox executives long suspected that some of its patented technologies were being illegally copied by other companies, no steps were taken to detect and stop such patent infringement. So moribund was Xerox's IP strategy, in fact, that the company reportedly earned only $8.5 million in patent license royalties in 1997. That's barely $1,000 per patent versus the $75,000 that each of IBM's 15,000 patents generated that same year, and a figure so low it didn't even cover the maintenance costs of the portfolio.

It was against this backdrop that Xerox recruited Rick Thoman, possibly the first Fortune 500 chief executive ever hired specifically (albeit certainly not solely) to maximize the value of a firm's intellectual property assets. "I've gotten full support from Paul [Allaire, Xerox's chairman]," Thoman is quick to point out. "And to Paul's credit, he's already done a lot to change this company—especially the shift to digital products. But intellectual property never really came up on his radar screen before because he never knew how much value could be generated from it. It was easier for me to see its importance, because when you come from IBM and you see patent revenues double in five years to hit $1 billion a year—and you also see how much leverage and negotiating power it gives you in the marketplace—you can't help but see it. So, yes, it was my idea to be aggressive in this space."

Since taking the helm, Thoman has carried out a restructuring program at Xerox that has helped the company push earnings growth back up into the low double-digits. But Thoman has also been busy working on the "intangible" side of things. In 1998, he formed Xerox Intellectual Property Operations, a new business unit run along profit and loss (P&L) lines, and hired Jan Jaferian as the company's first "Vice President of Intellectual Property." Under Thoman's guidance, Xerox is now developing an active patent licensing program, a more IP-savvy R&D effort, and a high-profile campaign against infringers that has already seen the company initiate several patent infringement lawsuits against major competitors such as Hewlett-Packard.

If the stakes are high—Thoman's own future as well as Xerox's hangs in the balance—the challenges, at least, are clear. "My job is to understand the nature of our technology advantage," he says, "and then use our intellectual property to leverage that advantage in the marketplace."

Will he succeed? Only time will tell, of course, but at least one Wall Street analyst believes Thoman's intellectual property revitalization effort has significant potential. "The fact that Xerox is now aggressively capitalizing on its intellectual property is extremely important," argues Daniel Kunstler, an analyst who covers Xerox for J.P. Morgan Securities. "It's a real change in how they're doing business, and I'd estimate it's going to be worth $10 to $15 per share to them over the period ahead."

In other words, if Kunstler is right, Rick Thoman's new IP strategy is going to increase the company's market capitalization by as much as 13 percent—or nearly $5 billion based on Xerox's stock price of $116 and market cap of $38 billion at the time of this writing.[2]

Kunstler's estimates may be too conservative, however, for he apparently assumes that Xerox's patent licensing revenues will only increase to about $60 million a year, or $7,500 per patent, which is barely one-tenth the per-patent revenue earned by IBM.[3] But what if Xerox instead is able to generate one-half the revenues per patent as IBM—a not impossible scenario? In that case, Thoman's new IP strategy could create $24 billion in new wealth for Xerox shareholders.

A NEW BREED OF CHIEF EXECUTIVE

Rick Thoman is part of a new breed of chief executive, a rising generation of business leaders who regard intellectual property management as a new core competency of the successful enterprise. Though still a minority among their peers, their companies are nonetheless among the most successful in the world. They are the market leaders, the dominant players, the "fast companies" such as Microsoft and Lucent, Intel and Dell, Dow Chemical and Gillette and Pfizer that today grace the covers of *Business Week* and *Barrons, Fortune* and *Forbes.*

These IP-savvy chief executives recognize that the burgeoning knowledge economy has given rise to a new ecology of competition in which the wars once fought for control of markets are now being waged over the exclusive rights to new ideas, innovations, and inventions. In this new ecology of competition, it is not land or natural resources but intellectual property that now carries the DNA of wealth creation, the genetic code for competitive advantage. For CEOs and other senior executives, therefore, survival of the fittest will mean mastering the secrets of intellectual property and, like modern-day alchemists, using these to turn knowledge into gold.

> **For CEOs, success requires mastering the secrets of intellectual property.**

Being skilled at turning knowledge into gold, of course, is not the *only* requirement for success. CEOs must still have a sharp eye for market trends, a keen ear for the voice of the customer, and a steady hand on the enterprise's operations. And in this respect, the Bill Gates, Andy Groves, Michael Dells, and Richard Thomans of our new knowledge economy have certainly done their share of reengineering and restructuring, downsizing and right-sizing. They have quality-managed and customer-focused, flattened their hierarchies and expanded their teams, reduced their cycle times and increased their inventory turns. But what distinguishes these executives is their understanding that all the change management campaigns in the world won't guarantee success—not without a strategy for wielding the levers of wealth creation. So just as the leveraged buyout kings of the 1970s and

1980s built empires atop the great overlooked asset of their time—real estate—this new breed of CEO seeks to capitalize on today's greatest unexploited asset: intellectual property.

Patent Strategy Becoming a Core Competency

The strategy and tactics of intellectual property management, of course, are still unfamiliar to most senior executives today. "Most CEOs today have risen to their positions without intellectual property rights ever being a significant factor in their success," observes IP consultant Mel Sharp, who orchestrated the legendary patent licensing campaign at Texas Instruments a decade ago that netted the firm $1.5 billion in revenues. "But I do not believe that CEOs will continue to be successful in the future unless they begin to look at intellectual property as critical to the success of their business."

Indeed, the challenge that executives face in coming to terms with the new strategic role of intellectual property is in many ways similar to that which they confronted earlier this decade in regard to information technology. Information technology was also once seen as a narrow "technical" function separate from overall business strategy. Now it is treated as a strategic factor in business success and an important element of the CEO's job.

"I think the same thing will happen with IP," suggests McKinsey & Company's Alberto Torres, a member of the consulting firm's intellectual asset management practice. "In the future, CEOs are going to have to become knowledgeable about intellectual property management. They are going to have to think about it as a major lever of value creation for the company."

The critical point here is that in today's knowledge economy, intellectual property can no longer be considered simply a legal function. Nor is it merely a matter of protecting your technologies or products from copying. It's about business strategy. *And that makes it the responsibility of the chief executive officer.*

THE CEO's CHALLENGE

How should chief executives exercise that responsibility? "Most CEOs today simply delegate IP matters to the patent lawyers," says former National Semiconductor and Apple CEO Gil Amelio, "and then the lawyers will go around and give a talk on patenting to a group of engineers at lunch or something. But it just goes in one ear and out the other. It's not a rigorous process. And the CEO is not providing leadership because he just doesn't see its importance."

Instead, the chief executive must take leadership, both in developing strategies that employ patents for competitive advantage and in creating the organizational structure needed to implement those strategies throughout the enterprise. We recognize, of course, that patent strategy is no Holy Grail for business success, nor is it a substitute for creating market-leading products, developing operational excellence, and conducting savvy marketing. But a strategic patent policy can significantly augment the CEO's ability to guide the enterprise to commercial success and increase shareholder return.

The Three Objectives of Patent Strategy

Indeed, a well-designed patent strategy can enable companies to:

Strengthen Proprietary Market Advantage

- Maintain product or service technology edge

- Boost R&D, branding, and market effectiveness

- Anticipate market and technology shifts

Improve Financial Performance

- Mine patent assets for new revenues

- Reduce costs

- Bolster corporate financing and valuation efforts

Enhance Competitiveness

- Outflank competitors

- Exploit new market opportunities

- Reduce competitive risks

CONDUCTING THE IP AUDIT

How does one actually develop an effective patent strategy? The first step is to get a handle on the size and strength of the patent assets themselves. This step may seem elementary, but as you will read in numerous case studies throughout this book, most firms have little or no idea of the commercial potential and financial value of their IP assets.

Dow Chemical was a case in point. Although historically aggressive in asserting its patents, Dow suffered in the past from a disorganized and ad hoc approach to IP management. Individual business units made their own decisions about the value and use of the patents created in their division, and there existed no structure or method for assessing and maximizing the patents' value to the enterprise as a whole, either as revenue-generating assets or as competitive weapons.

"It used to be just two people in licensing," recalls Sam Khoury, who was a leader of the team that revolutionized Dow's use of its patent assets before leaving the firm to take on the presidency of the IP management firm Consor. "If the phone rang, they answered it. And if it didn't, they just sat back and read the *Wall Street Journal.*"

In the early 1990s, however, an industry-wide recession forced Dow to cut back on expenditures. During one meeting of the board of directors, R&D chief Fred Courson was asked by board members to quantify the return on the $1 billion a year that the firm was then spending on research. He couldn't do it.

"They really slapped him around," Khoury laughs. "And he came out of that meeting vowing he would never again walk into a board meeting unprepared. He said from now on he wanted to know everything about our intellectual property."

Thus began a year-long audit of IP assets at Dow—new automated technology tools can now reduce this time to days—that would later become something of a legend in intellectual property circles. Each of the company's 29,000 patents was identified, valued, and assigned to one of 15 major business units, which thereafter assumed financial responsibility for its use. A new structure was also put into place in which "intellectual asset managers" from the various business units would meet regularly to review patent activity on an enterprise-wide basis. The Intellectual Asset Management team's job was to identify licensing, commercialization, or joint venture opportunities for individual patents or groups of patents, as well as to target competitive gaps in the portfolio as a whole that needed attention.

"We used to meet once a month, and I think they still do," says Khoury. "And other than your own death, there was no excuse for not attending. We also met with three members of the board on a monthly basis, which shows you how importantly the top leadership viewed this process."

And no wonder, considering that simply by conducting this IP audit, Dow achieved an immediate savings of $50 million in taxes and maintenance fees on unneeded patents that were pruned from the portfolio and either abandoned or donated to universities and nonprofit groups. What's more, since the audit was completed in 1994, patent licensing revenues have skyrocketed from $25 million to more than $125 million today. According to Gordon Petrash, the former director of the Intellectual Asset Management program at Dow who has since joined the consulting firm PriceWaterhouseCoopers, if you factor in the commercial benefits from more effectively aligning the firm's technology assets with its business goals, the audit probably also produced "billions and billions" in new revenues.

Creating the IP Audit Map

So how can your company conduct an IP audit? First assign each of your patents to a business unit that either already employs the patented technology in its products or services or intends to do so in the future. Next, create a grid map in which the business units are grouped along the vertical axis according to their growth rate compared with a standard metric. We like to use the gross domestic product (GDP) of the country in which the business operates as the standard metric because it normalizes the growth rates of units operating in different countries. Business units are thus grouped according to whether they are growing at, say, four or more times the GDP growth rate of the country of operation, two to four times the GDP growth rate, or the same rate as the GDP. Finally, along the horizontal axis, group the patents according to whether they are integral to products in the unit's current operating plan, in a future strategic plan, or in no plan at all.

Now you have a basic map showing in broad outlines which patents have the greatest and most direct commercial value, which might be more suitable for licensing out to generate revenues, and which should simply be abandoned to reduce the costs of maintaining the portfolio.

In Dow's case (Figure 3-1), 51 percent of Dow's patents fell into the most valuable upper-left quadrant of the chart, as these had direct application in the commercial activities of its higher-growth business units. Another 36 percent of the patents fell into the upper-right quadrant of the map, representing IP assets that had no direct use in current or planned products but might nevertheless be valuable to other firms engaged in related high-growth businesses. It was on these neglected but potentially valuable patents that Dow's Intellectual Asset Management team concentrated its revenue-generating licensing efforts. The final 13 percent of Dow's patents fell into the lower-right quadrant of the audit map, representing technologies that were not being used by the firm's business units and were unlikely to be valuable to other companies. These were abandoned.

THE GROW-FIX-SELL TRIAGE

Once you have assessed in general terms the strength and value of your patents, you can now develop strategies that leverage this strength and value for competitive gain. And the best place to begin, of course, is with the chief executive. Consider, for exam-

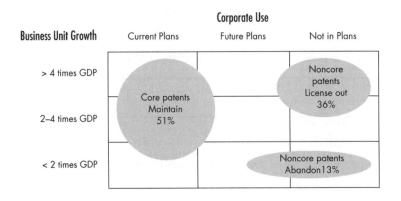

FIGURE 3-1   DOW CHEMICAL IP AUDIT MAP

ple, the CEO's basic task—which is to build, prune, and sustain a high economic value-added (EVA) business or portfolio of businesses in order to increase shareholder return. This means looking at the current performance and future prospects of each of the business units within the company and then determining which have the greatest growth potential and should receive the greatest share of corporate investment and resources, which are either underperforming or perhaps still embryonic but nonetheless have significant potential, and which are simply a drain on enterprise resources and should be shut down or sold off.

Essentially, it's a triage process—we call it the Grow-Fix-Sell triage—in which the CEO is constantly making decisions about which businesses the company should devote long-range efforts toward growing, which need immediate fixing, and which should be abandoned. By looking through the clarifying lens of intellectual property, the CEO can gain new insights and open up new strategy options for managing this Grow-Fix-Sell triage process successfully.

As you can see in Figure 3-2, the patent strategies employed by an enterprise's business units will vary greatly depending on their position on our Grow-Fix-Sell triage map. Although the growth rate of each business unit certainly influences its position on this triage map, this rate is only one of several factors that determine whether any particular business needs a grow-, fix-, or sell-oriented patent strategy. Market share, the strength and strategies of your competitors, and the phase of industry growth—for example, is it an emerging or a maturing business?—also shape the IP strategy needs of each business unit. In fact, the Grow-Fix-Sell triage is not so much a classification scheme as it is a set of strategy approaches, each with its own timeline, competitive challenges, and patent utilization goals. An underperforming business unit, for example, may need both a short-term Fix strategy to stabilize falling margins as well as a long-term Grow strategy to develop new product lines or expand into new markets.

IP-Enabled "Grow" Strategies

As a general rule, IP-enhanced Grow strategies typically deal with long-term issues such as the development of new product lines or expansion into new markets. Where does the firm need to go next? What new products are needed down the road? What are the long-term plans and capabilities of competitors? Are there any significant market or technology shifts in the offing? If so,

---

FIGURE 3-2   USING PATENT STRATEGY IN THE GROW-FIX-SELL TRIAGE

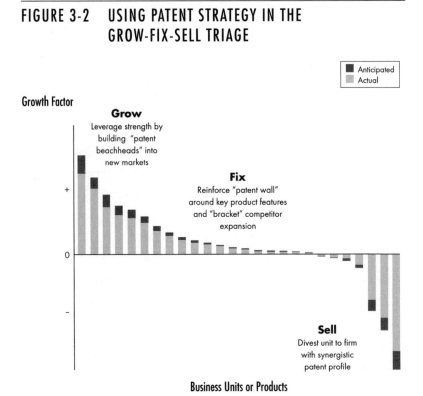

what enabling technologies will the company need to build, license, or acquire—and what partnerships will it need to forge—in order to take advantage of those shifts?

All these questions focus on the firm's competitive position 18 months to 5 years in the future. And all have the strategic aim of protecting that future, of making sure that the firm is not precluded from being able to exploit tomorrow's biggest revenue and growth opportunities.

Cisco's aggressive efforts in recent years to acquire companies with telephony-related technology patents is an example of an M&A Grow strategy aimed at preparing the company to compete head-to-head with Lucent (which is trying to extend its own dominance in voice networking to the data arena that Cisco has traditionally ruled). Texas Instruments (TI) also employed a patent-driven M&A Grow strategy when it acquired Amati Communications in 1997 for the staggering sum of $395 million (see Chapter 6). The acquisition was motivated in part by TI's belief that the modem business was shifting to high-speed DSL (Digital Subscriber Line) technology; thus, the company moved to lock up Amati's 25 seminal DSL patents and fortify its long-term ability to compete in that space.

Patent Grow strategies are aimed at protecting the company's future.

The $3.5 billion Avery Dennison Corporation offers another example of an IP-enabled Grow strategy at work. In 1994, one of Avery's embryonic business units developed a new film for use in product labeling. This unit had already won an important contract to provide the labels for Procter & Gamble shampoo bottles and was thought to have considerable growth potential. An analysis of other companies' patent activity, however, indicated that Dow Chemical was also beginning to move into the business. Should Avery commit the huge resources needed to exploit the market opportunity for the film unit, especially when it looked as if Dow might become a formidable competitor?

Paul Germeraad, the former vice president and director of corporate research at Avery Dennison and vice president of the Industrial Research Institute (which represents the largest corporate R&D organizations in the United States), describes what happened.[4] "We saw that we had the more fundamental patents in this area," he recalls, "and we strengthened those with additional patent filings. Then, with the support of the CEO, we went to Dow and basically told them that they couldn't manufacture their film anymore. They had to shut down their team, dismantle it, and withdraw from the market. And that's exactly what Dow did. Thanks to the strength of our patents—and our CEO's willingness, based on that IP strength, to bet our total resources on building this unit—we were able to stop Dow in the market and have it basically all to ourselves. And as a result, that unit became one of the fastest-growing, highest-EVA units in the company."

In other words, looking through the lens of intellectual property enabled Avery Dennison to take a fast-growing but potentially vulnerable business and, by reinforcing the patent wall around it and threatening archcompetitor Dow with costly infringement action, protect and expand it.

Eastman Chemical, on the other hand, offers an example of the losses that can result from the failure to employ an IP-enhanced Grow strategy when it is needed. In the early 1980s, Eastman owned two of the fundamental patents related to polyethylene terephthalate (PET), which is used to make soft-drink bottles. It was a high-growth business, but the firm failed to leverage its early market strength either by creating a reinforcing patent wall around those two core patents or by establishing patent beachheads into related new markets. The ever-aggressive Dow, meanwhile, took advantage of Eastman's patent passivity and expanded its own portfolio of PET patents into a variety of related business sectors. In the end, Eastman left a huge revenue opportunity on the table, which Dow happily picked up.

IP Tools for "Grow" Strategies. Eastman Chemical's failure to leverage its early patent strength in the PET business highlights the need to carefully analyze the patent landscape when assessing new product or market opportunities. A variety of techniques for data mining and visualizing patent information can help you accomplish this task, including a simple Patent Hit Count by Year, which will show you whether the technologies central to your proposed product or service offering are heading up or down in importance, as well as how many and which other players are pursuing potentially competitive development efforts. Are more or fewer patents being granted in the technology? Is the pace of development accelerating or slowing? Are there unexpected patent assignees involved who might be future competitors? Are there any strategic "choke points" in the enabling technologies that you can patent in order to secure a proprietary advantage?

Figure 3-3a illustrates the rapid growth of technology development in the e-commerce auction business, for example. Anyone reading the newspaper, of course, would be well aware of the extensive activity in this field, but only patent analysis can unearth unlikely or hidden potential competitors (such as the Reuters and Cantor Fitzgerald Securities patent applications shown in Figure 3-3b) that may be planning to launch ventures in the auction arena. And only by drilling down to a more detailed analysis of the patents involved can you determine if your own embryonic auction business may be treading on already-patented aspects of e-commerce auction technology.

In point of fact, shortly after the paragraph above was written, Cantor Fitzgerald filed a patent infringement suit against Liberty Brokerage Investment corporation alleging that its patented electronic auction trading protocol had been infringed by Liberty. Given the explosive growth of the on-line auction business, this suit promises to be only the first of many patent battles to come in this critical e-commerce sector. According to Forrester Research, $65 billion in transactions will take place via business-to-business and consumer auctions on the Net by 2002. And a host of vendors, both small start-ups as well as industry leaders such as IBM and Microsoft, are rushing prepackaged auction software systems to market so that auction businesses won't have to continue building their own technology in house.

Another IP tool that is especially useful in analyzing emerging fields such as e-commerce is a topographical or IP Landscape Map, which can reveal the terrain of competition along a variety of parameters. It can show where your competitors are spending the most R&D money over time, for instance. Or it can spot areas of increased technology development in a nascent industry, as in

FIGURE 3-3a U.S. COMPUTER AUCTION PATENTS BY YEAR

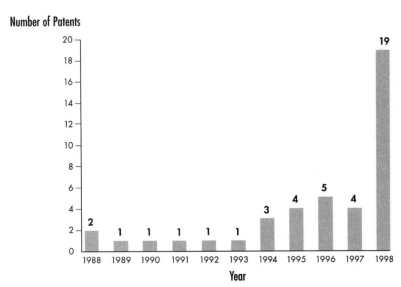

Number of Patents

Source: Courtesy of Aurigin Systems, Inc.

the map of patenting activity in the e-commerce sector shown in Figure 3-4.

As the detail window at the left of the map in Figure 3-4 shows, there are 351 patents classified as "Postage Meter" patents and 152 as "Postal" patents. In addition, there are also 279 "Mail" patents (not shown), for a total of 782 postage/mail/meter patents (actually 520 after subtracting duplicates). Pitney-Bowes holds the lion's share—283, to be precise—of these 520 patents in Internet-related postage and mail technologies. Was upstart competitor eStamp, with only 8 patents of its own in this field, even aware of which specific technologies were covered by Pitney-Bowes's hefty patent position? Did it try to avoid infringing those patents in developing its own technology? All that we know at this point is that the two companies are currently

FIGURE 3-3b COMPUTER AUCTION PATENT APPLICATION REPORT BY YEAR

	1991	1992	1993	1994	1995	1996	1997	1998
Cantor Fitzgerald Securities			1					1
Cybergold, Inc.							1	
Fisher, Alan S.							1	
Fitts, Gary							1	
Goldhaber, A. Nathaniel							1	
Hauser, Ralph Christian							1	
Hitachi, Ltd.								1
International Business Machines Corporation							1	1
Kaplan, Samuel Jerroll							1	
Mitsubishi Corporation				1	1			1
News Datacom, Ltd.			1					
Nieaf-Smitt B.V.			1					
Onsale, Inc.							1	
Rueters, Ltd.	1							
Summit Telecom Systems, Inc.								1
Symbol Technologies, Inc.								1
Tsudik, Gene							1	
Walker Asset Management								1

Source: Courtesy of Aurigin Systems, Inc.

FIGURE 3-4 IP LANDSCAPE MAP: U.S. E-COMMERCE PATENTS

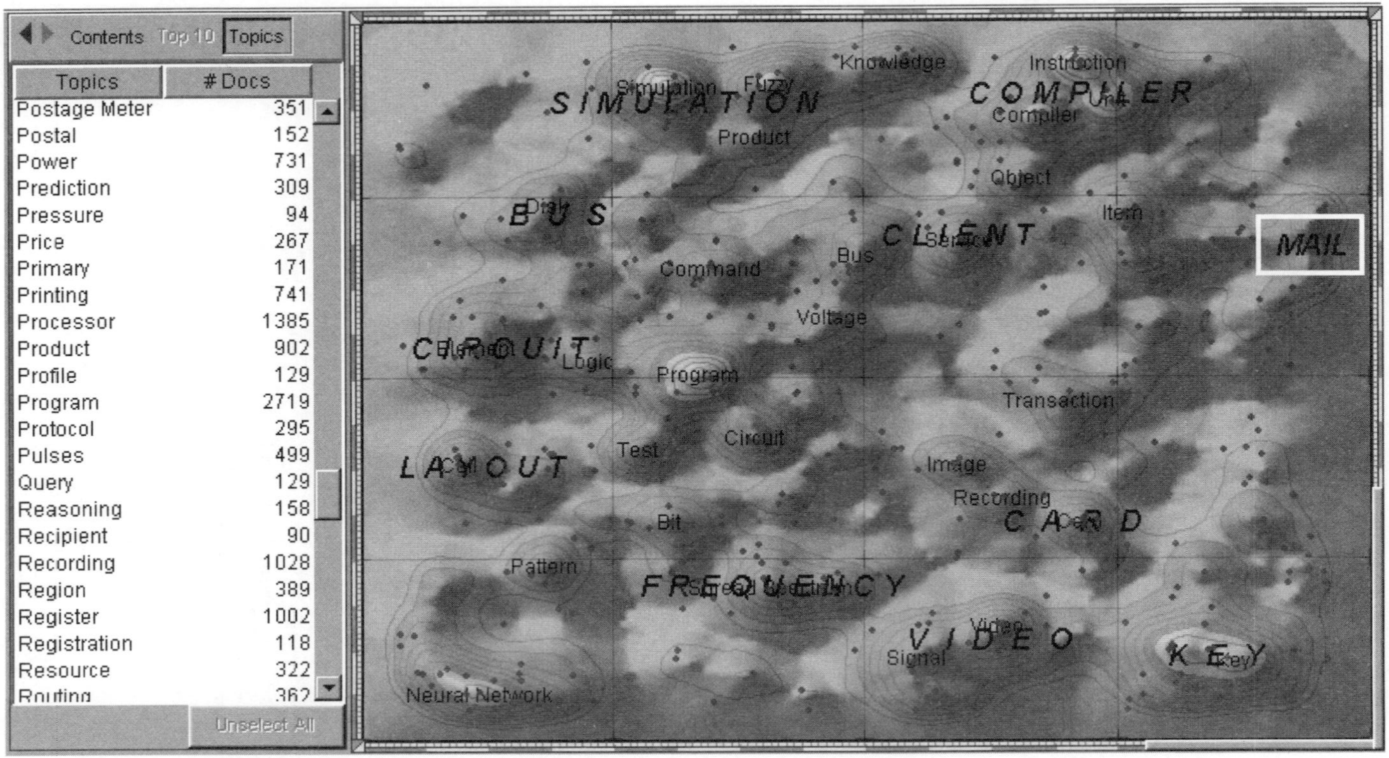

Topics	# Docs
Postage Meter	351
Postal	152
Power	731
Prediction	309
Pressure	94
Price	267
Primary	171
Printing	741
Processor	1385
Product	902
Profile	129
Program	2719
Protocol	295
Pulses	499
Query	129
Reasoning	158
Recipient	90
Recording	1028
Region	389
Register	1002
Registration	118
Resource	322
Routing	362

Source: Chart courtesy of Aurigin Systems, Inc., using ThemeScape™ software module.

negotiating a possible patent cross-licensing agreement. But if these negotiations fail, eStamp could find itself embroiled in a very costly patent suit with its much larger, $4 billion competitor.

[And once again, reality has overtaken the authors' speculations. Shortly after the above paragraph was written, negotiations between the two parties broke off and Pitney-Bowes filed a patent infringement suit against eStamp in a Delaware U.S. District Court.]

Other IP analysis tools that help you assess the direction and strength of your competitors' technology plans may also prove useful in developing effective Grow strategies. An Innovation Cycle Speed report, for example, can show how rapidly your competitor is moving to develop a new technology by charting the median age of its patents' prior art citations, which are references to any earlier or related technologies that the patented invention has improved upon or designed around. If the Innovation Cycle Speed report indicates that your competitor is rapidly citing its own earlier patents, it could mean it has a core technology and is moving quickly to develop major products based on it. If the report additionally shows that this competitor is also rapidly citing *your* patents as well, this could indicate that it is working on products that may be very similar to yours and trying to get to market first.

IP-Enhanced "Fix" Strategies

In contrast to the longer-term directional issues addressed by IP Grow strategies, patent-enhanced Fix strategies usually deal with issues of slowing growth, cluttered markets, falling profits, eroding margins, and commoditization. What higher-margin product line extensions might enable a company to increase profitability? Are there unexploited revenue sources that could be tapped without much expense? How can one de-commoditize what is fast becoming a mature business? Fix strategies typically deal with here-and-now problems and offer solutions that typically require no more than 12 to 18 months to implement. Their strategic goal is usually to defend margins, boost incremental revenue, and better position the company to take advantage of new growth opportunities.

The Japanese company Canon, for example, employed an IP-based Fix strategy in the product development program for its copier business a few years ago. Canon had established an early market strength in inkjet printers, but as competition began to drive margins down to 10 percent or below, the company saw an opportunity to patent a family of inkjet cartridges, paper supplies, and other consumables. These consumables today earn margins of more than 50 percent.

Patent Fix strategies can defend your margins and increase incremental revenue.

Eroding margins were also partly to blame for the 1999 firing of Compaq Computer's CEO over his failure to build a direct sales business over the Internet. IBM faced the same problem in early 1999—its PC business was running at a loss—but in contrast to Compaq, it engineered an IP Fix that may help it launch its own high-margin direct sales effort. Big Blue cross-licensed its patent portfolio with Dell's in a deal that gives Dell royalty-free access to the IBM components it needs while giving IBM access to the patented manufacturing, marketing, and distribution technologies that Dell employs in running its world-leading direct sales operation.

Apple Computer also employed an IP-based Fix strategy in 1997 when, faced with crumbling market share and paralysis in its software development efforts, the company settled a patent dispute with Microsoft in exchange for $150 million and Microsoft's promise to continue supporting its Microsoft Office application software for the Macintosh for a minimum of five more years. This not only eliminated a threat to Apple's long-term future—without Microsoft Office software, there would be little use for either the new Mac OS 8 operating system or the speedy new G3 machines that are the basis for Apple's turnaround—but in the short term also gave Apple the time it needed to restore profitability and bring out the hot-selling iMac and other new products.

IP Tools for "Fix" Strategies. One of the most powerful tools for developing an effective IP-based Fix strategy involves tapping the asset value of your patent portfolio itself. Chapter 5, for example, shows how a Patent Citation Tree can help identify potential targets for a patent licensing program aimed at generating new revenues. But another problem businesses increasingly face these days is the recruitment and retention of key engineering talent. An Inventor Report will tell you who the leading inventors are in your technology field and show you their employment patterns—including their past willingness to change jobs for a better offer.

Figure 3-5, for example, shows that a Mr. Stephen Tyler Carroll is one of the more prolific inventors in e-commerce auction technology. But Mr. William A. Lupien might actually be a better candidate for recruitment. For one thing, an analysis of his patents (not shown) indicates that he may have worked on a broader range of auction technologies. And for another, Figure 3-5 also shows a willingness on Mr. Lupien's part to change jobs—he worked first for Lattice Investments and then joined Optimark Technologies. Searching one of the Web directories such as PeopleFinder or WhoWhere ought to turn up his phone number. But if not, you can always call him at Optimark,

FIGURE 3-5   INVENTOR REPORT FOR E-COMMERCE AUCTIONS

Inventor Name	Assignee	Document Count
Carroll, Stephen Tyler	Papyrus Technology Corp.	3 **3**
O'Neill, Desmond Sean	Papyrus Technology Corp.	3 **3**
Patterson, Jr., L. Thomas	Papyrus Technology Corp.	3 **3**
Fitts, Gary	Cybergold, Inc.	2 **2**
Fujisaki, Masataka	Aucnet Inc. Flex Japan Inc.	1 1 **2**
Ginsberg, Philip Myron	Cantor Fitzgerald & Co., Inc.	2 **2**
Goldhaber, A. Nathaniel	Cybergold, Inc.	2 **2**
Hollander, Richard	Tandy Corporation	2 **2**
Jorasch, James A.	Walker Asset Management Limited Partnership	2 **2**
Keller, Norman	Reuters Limited	2 **2**
Lupien, William A.	Lattice Investments, Inc. Optimark Technologies, Inc.	1 1 **2**
Roach, John V.	Tandy Corporation	2 **2**
Schneier, Bruce	Walker Asset Management Limited Partnership	2 **2**
Silverman, David L.	Reuters Limited	2 **2**
Walker, Jay S.	Walker Asset Management Limited Partnership	2 **2**

Source: Courtesy of Aurigin Systems, Inc.

assuming your CEO has given the go-ahead to make Mr. Lupien a generous offer.

Incidentally, finding top technical talent is not the only challenge CEOs and their human resource and R&D managers face these days. *Keeping* their best inventors is a task of equal if not greater importance. The Japanese electronics giant JVC, for example, recently announced that it will begin paying employees up to $825,000 for each invention that leads to a new patent. If your company wishes to initiate its own employee retention program, you might want to begin with a Patent Count by Inventor that spotlights your most prolific inventors so you can target them for a pair of "golden handcuffs" or other special treatment.

Figure 3-6, for example, lists the most prolific inventors at Microsoft. Do Microsoft managers know who these engineers are—and is the company doing everything it can to make sure they remain with the firm? Given Microsoft's aggressive patenting policies in recent years, we wouldn't be surprised if Bill Gates himself keeps a chart like this somewhere on his desk.

Patent-Enabled "Sell" Strategies

All Sell strategies are based on the ancient axiom that one man's junk is another man's treasure. When your margins have evaporated, your competitors have outflanked you, all your Fix strategies have failed, and the market is simply against you, it's time to quit. Sell strategies typically deal with a time frame of yesterday (as in, "We should have gotten out of this revenue sinkhole long ago") and their strategic goal is to get the most economic or strategic value from the sale of a dying business.

Avery Dennison employed an IP-enabled Sell strategy a few

FIGURE 3-6   PATENT COUNT BY INVENTOR: MICROSOFT

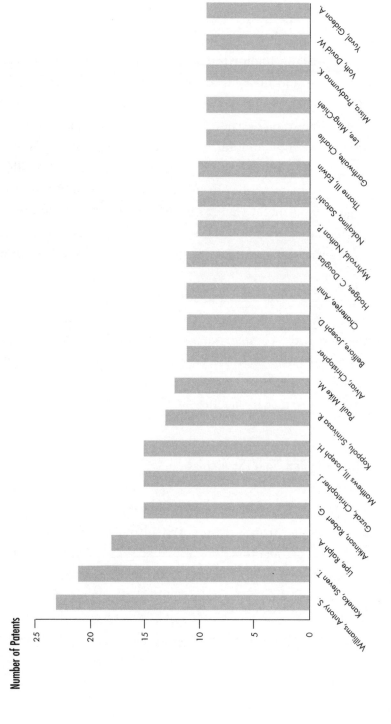

Number of Patents

Source: Courtesy of Aurigin Systems, Inc.

years ago to turn a slowly dying business unit into a major growth opportunity. The company had been struggling over what to do with a mature business that, though still generating revenue, had slowed dramatically in growth. Analysis of the patent landscape surrounding this business revealed that any further growth of the unit would be severely constrained because the market had be-

Patent Sell strategies follow the ancient axiom that one man's junk is another's treasure.

come cluttered with competitors who had surrounded Avery's patents with strong IP positions of their own.

What did the company do? "We sold off that business, including the patents, and reinvested that money into the Duracell label program, which was just beginning to show explosive growth," explains Germeraad. "From a revenue standpoint, it may have looked like an even trade. But we swapped a mature, low-growth business for a higher-EVA growth business with much greater upside."

IP Tools for "Sell" Strategies. Since the principal challenge in any Sell strategy is to find a company that would find your business of value, the goal in analyzing the patent landscape is to find companies with a patent profile that is synergistic with your own. A Patent Citation Tree will show which companies are citing your patents in theirs and therefore might be interested in acquiring your patents.

Figure 3-7 shows that Samsung (in the lower-left corner) has a small patent position in MPEG video compression technology, and that Sony has cited some of Samsung's patents in its own MPEG efforts. Neither company has the strength of Intel or IBM, so if Samsung wanted to sell, then Sony might be a logical candidate.

FIGURE 3-7　PATENT CITATION TREE: MPEG TECHNOLOGY FROM IBM PATENT

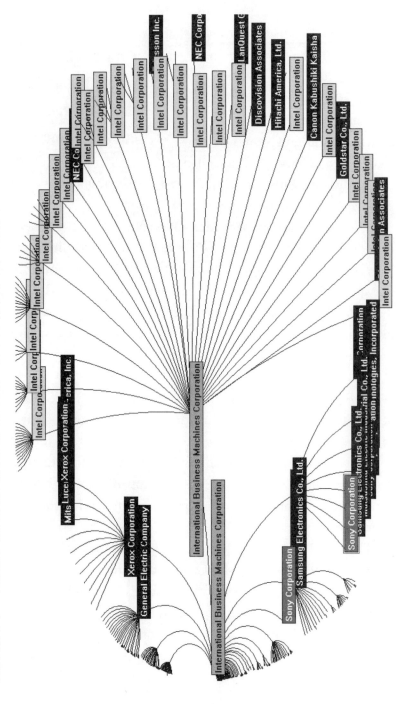

Source: Courtesy of Aurigin Systems, Inc.

BUILDING THE IP-SAVVY ORGANIZATION

It's one thing to brainstorm a bunch of new strategies, of course, and quite another to build the organizational structure needed to execute them well. As noted earlier, the CEO's challenge is not only to take the lead in developing patent strategies but also to ensure there is an organizational structure that can drive IP strategy implementation through every business unit and functional group within the enterprise, from R&D and marketing to finance, mergers and acquisitions, and e-commerce.

Hence, every CEO must ask himself or herself the following question: Does our management structure reflect the strategic importance of intellectual property to enterprise success?

For the vast majority of businesses in America and around the world, the answer to this question would have to be no. Most businesses today still concentrate patent responsibilities in the legal department—the one group in the firm, ironically, that is specifically *not* trained to make business decisions. The problem with this approach becomes apparent when you imagine attorneys being given any sort of

Does your management structure reflect the strategic importance of intellectual property?

similar responsibility for the disposition of a firm's tangible assets. When General Motors considers whether to buy a parcel of land and build a new manufacturing facility, for example, is it the lawyers who discuss the likely competitive effects or the return on investment of the purchase and make the final decision? No, that's the job of the business and finance executives. The legal department's job is simply to make sure that title to the land is free of encumbrances and that the deal is structured properly.

Yet when it comes to managing their intangible (and in most cases, far more valuable) intellectual property assets, most companies still leave it either to the lawyers or to the individual business units. The result, in the words of *CEO* magazine, is that "IP assets are not visible above the division level and the company as a whole does not know how to identify or properly value its intellectual property."[5]

The New IP-Savvy Xerox

At Xerox, however, a new organizational structure has been developed under CEO Rick Thoman's leadership. All its intellectual property assets have now been centralized in the newly formed Xerox Intellectual Property Operations (XIPO) unit, which has P&L responsibility for managing the company's huge patent portfolio. XIPO is headed by the vice president of intellectual property, Jan Jaferian, but the unit itself is overseen by the company's top strategy-making group, which includes Richard Thoman, company chairman Paul Allaire, R&D chief Mark Myers, Executive Vice President of Business Operations Bill Buehler, CFO Barry Romeril, and customer operations chief Barry Rand.

This new leadership structure reflects Thoman's view that determining the competitive and financial uses of a company's intellectual property assets is among the principal responsibilities of top leadership. It also helps ensure that IP strategy is developed with the interests of the entire organization in mind, for patents are no longer considered the property of the individual business units where they are created but rather the assets of the whole corporation.

"Just like we say that different business units create cash but the cash belongs to the corporation, that's how we now view our intellectual property," explains R&D chief Mark Myers. "This enables us to make better choices about product development, and it also avoids a lot of problems, too."

Previously, for example, a research team in a business unit might have started designing a product only to discover, far downstream in the process, that they had stumbled onto a potential infringement problem or that they needed to license someone else's technology to complete the product's development. Myers calls this the "Oops Factor"—when a lack of foresight, proper early-stage planning, or the ability to survey the company's needs as a whole can end up costing time, money, or a loss of competitive position.

"It has certainly happened before that a team will get down the road and suddenly go, 'Oops!'" he explains. "Then they complain that unless they can trade off some of our technology to get what they need to finish the project, they'll have to take a schedule delay or spend another $20 million to design around the problem. Well, it used to be that they'd make that decision for themselves, and possibly trade out a valuable group of patents to keep their project going. And naturally, when you're caught between a rock and a hard place like that, the people you're negotiating with can smell it. They can see you perspiring. So you always lose.

"But now," he notes, "we decide that centrally—and, just as important, we decide it in the early stages of R&D, before we've gotten entrapped in problems, and where we still have a lot more choices. In cases such as the one I just described, we may decide that the patents they want to trade could generate more money in licensing fees if kept in-house than it would cost us to design our own solution internally. Or, looking at the larger technology trends in the industry, we may decide that those patents aren't all that valuable either for licensing or for the longer-term strategic needs of the company after all, so we'll trade them out."

A Question of Structure

The bottom line here is that companies must create an organizational structure that is conducive to assessing and making strategic decisions about intellectual property on an enterprise-wide basis. For companies such as Xerox and Lucent, this has meant creating an intellectual property business unit with P&L responsibility for managing patents as corporate-wide assets and generating a return on those assets. Other companies may find Dow's use of an "Intellectual Asset Management" team composed of patent liaisons from all the business units more appropriate. Still others, especially smaller firms, will decide that the liaisons should come from the enterprise's functional units—R&D, product development, marketing, finance, and business development (including M&A)—rather than from the business units or divisions, especially if they don't have multiple divisions.

Figures 3-8a and 3-8b contrast the old and new approaches to organizing IP management within a firm. Under the old approach (Figure 3-8a), the R&D unit produced inventions, which were then handled by the legal department for prosecution of patents. Trade secrets and issued patents were then typically stored in the legal department's file cabinet, where access to them was limited to the legal staff, using mostly paper-based methods. In contrast, the new approach to IP management (Figure 3-8b) employs a more open structure. IP knowledge is captured and shared via computerized technology and is available on an enterprise-wide basis to every business unit and functional team in the company, from R&D and finance to the business development and M&A staff. Corporate IP is thus more fully exploited and protected. In short, IP is treated not just as a legal instrument, but as a corporate asset and strategic business tool of potentially great importance to the firm's competitive success.

But however the IP management effort is organized, three

requirements must be met by any company that wishes to put their patents to work for profit and competitive advantage:

1. *Reporting* of patent creation and usage must reside in the business unit to encourage P&L management of intellectual property as business assets for which a return is expected.

2. *Oversight* of IP strategy and deployment must rise above the business units and be centralized at the top executive level in order to serve the needs of the whole enterprise.

3. *Leadership* must be placed in the hands of a senior, vice-president-level (if not board-level) executive with enterprise-wide authority.

The last point is nonnegotiable. There is simply no way to treat intellectual property as a strategic asset unless responsibility for it is shouldered by someone with the authority to make strategic enterprise-wide decisions.

Where the Buck Stops

But even these three requirements are not enough. As *CEO* magazine noted, "One of the biggest mistakes that CEOs make is to vest responsibility for intellectual property issues in others and then assume they are being managed. Without a CEO who understands IP issues and can focus and motivate vigorous [activity around] intellectual property, management of IP can easily falter."[6]

Dr. Mildred Hastbacka of Arthur D. Little consulting has studied the process by which companies finally "get religion" about intellectual property. Apparently, putting a company's IP assets to work for profit and competitive advantage does not require any large-scale change management movements,

FIGURE 3-8a   OLD IP ORGANIZATION CHART

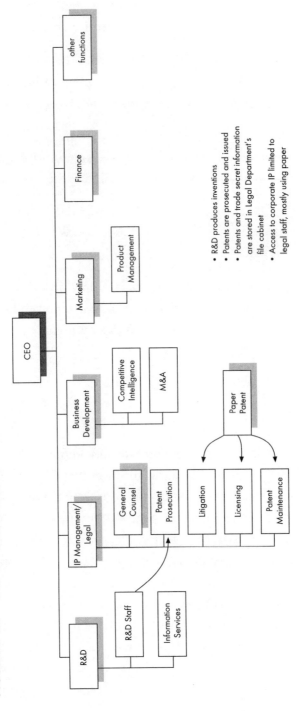

- R&D produces inventions
- Patents are prosecuted and issued
- Patents and trade secret information are stored in Legal Department's file cabinet
- Access to corporate IP limited to legal staff, mostly using paper

FIGURE 3-8b STRATEGIC IP ORGANIZATION

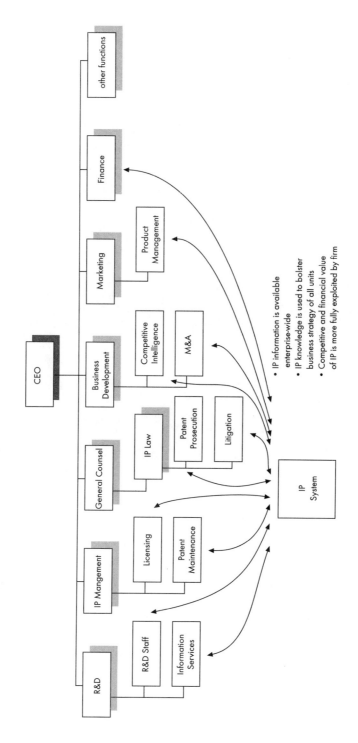

- IP information is available enterprise-wide
- IP knowledge is used to bolster business strategy of all units
- Competitive and financial value of IP is more fully exploited by firm

business process reengineering campaigns, or other corporate voodoo. In fact, there doesn't seem to be any great mystery to it at all.

"At some point," explains Dr. Hastbacka, "a decision is made, typically by the CEO, that the company is going to begin using its intellectual assets in a way that is significantly different from the way it had been using them. In other words, the CEO [simply decides] to maximize return on *all* assets, including intellectual assets."[7]

It is precisely at this point that those obscure little pieces of paper called patents become Rembrandts in the attic.

officers, agents, servants, employees, and attorneys and those persons in active concert and participation with them [must] stop manufacturing, using and selling [instant] cameras and film."[5] It would take another five years of legal wrangling (and mounting attorneys' fees) before the damages phase of the trial was finally resolved in 1990.

The total cost to Kodak of its misguided patent strategy? The company was ordered to pay Polaroid a staggering $925 million in damages. Kodak was also forced to shut down its $1.5 billion manufacturing plant, lay off 700 workers, and spend nearly $500 million to buy back the 16 million instant cameras it had sold to consumers between 1976 and 1985. Legal fees during the 14-year-long court battle cost Kodak an additional $100 million. And a decades-long R&D effort had to be completely abandoned, written off as a total loss.

Today, all that remains of Kodak's aborted venture in the instant photography business are a few thousand unreturned cameras—collector's items for the serious hobbyist, and testaments to the terrible retribution that can befall a company when it disregards the central role that intellectual property must play in shaping R&D strategy.

BUILDING YOUR COMPANY'S FUTURE

The Kodak debacle, if nothing else, is a dramatic reminder of the extraordinary stakes involved in large-scale R&D projects. These are often "bet the company" affairs, after all, that put enormous capital and strategic investments at great risk. A failure to properly address IP issues in R&D can lead to catastrophic losses, not only in infringement costs but in the loss of market share, margin erosion, and reduced competitiveness in the market.

As the midwife of your company's future, however, R&D can

4

SUPERCHARGING R&D
THROUGH PATENT PLANNING

Sometimes the only thing standing between a blockbuster hit product and a multibillion-dollar market catastrophe is a single piece of paper. In the case of Eastman Kodak, it was actually seven pieces of paper—the claims pages of seven patents owned by Kodak archrival Polaroid—that led to the costliest R&D disaster in American business history. Those seven patents brought about the total destruction of Kodak's instant photography business, at a cost to the company of more than $3 billion in infringement damages, legal fees, and wasted R&D and manufacturing costs.

The origins of the Kodak debacle go back, as they so often do in such matters, to key decisions made in the early stages of the R&D process itself. In the early 1960s, Kodak was engaged in small-scale research to develop cameras and film for the instant photography market, which was wholly dominated at the time by the Polaroid Corporation, a company with only one-tenth Kodak's $10 billion in annual sales. But these research efforts failed to yield any products of sufficient quality to compete with Polaroid's and were quietly abandoned. By the late 1960s, however, Polaroid's instant camera sales had exploded to the point where they represented 15 percent of all camera purchases in the United States, and Kodak's top management reportedly became obsessed with the idea of grabbing a piece of the action. As one observer who has written about the case noted, "The idea of muscling in on what was becoming a lucrative business that the much smaller Polaroid company had all to itself must have been irresistible."[1]

So in 1969, Kodak launched a renewed, all-out research effort code-named "Project 130" to develop instant cameras and films. But given the failure of its previous research and the clear superiority of Polaroid technology, Kodak apparently felt it had little choice but to pursue technologies that arguably bore at least some similarity to those already successfully developed by Polaroid. There's nothing inherently wrong, of course, with pursuing technology approaches that are similar to those of one's competitors. Indeed, the reason patents are required to be publicly disclosed is precisely so that inventors can build on and ultimately leapfrog the discoveries of previous patent holders with new and more advanced inventions of their own. The key question here is whether one has created a unique new innovation, or has instead merely copied, and thus infringed upon, the work of others.

Kodak's senior executives and R&D managers clearly knew of the potential infringement dangers that might arise from following in Polaroid's footsteps. For one thing, Polaroid was fanatical about surrounding its products with patents —"We referred to [Polaroid] as a patent thicket," recalled one senior Kodak researcher.[2] Also, Polaroid had already shown some of its secret next-generation product designs to Kodak under the terms of an earlier joint development agreement between the two companies.

Because of these concerns, Kodak hired a respected New York law firm to advise its R&D department on patent matters. Written instructions were issued to Kodak technical staff stating that they "should not be constrained by what an individual feels is potential patent infringement"—a sentence that would later come back to haunt Kodak in court—but should instead refer all questions to the patent attorneys. But Kodak's efforts to limit its potential infringement liability were ultimately undermined by a fundamental flaw in its patent strategy: the company's R&D was directed not so much toward designing around the Polaroid patents as toward having those patents ruled invalid if the company was ever challenged in court. Explained Cecil D. Quillen, Jr., the patent attorney assigned by Kodak to its instant photography R&D effort: "There were a number of Polaroid patents that we thought under the legal standards of the day should have been ruled invalid."[3]

Maybe so. But would you bet your entire business on the rather risky hope that, once dragged into court and sued, you could overturn the already-issued patents of your accuser? Blinded by greed, hubris, and no small amount of self-delusion, the giant Eastman Kodak company was apparently willing to do just that.[4]

And so on April 20, 1976, Kodak launched its new line of instant cameras and films to the accompaniment of the largest advertising campaign in the history of the consumer photo business. Seven days later and to no one's surprise—instant photography, after all, represented 90 percent of Polaroid's $1 billion in annual sales—Polaroid responded with a lawsuit charging Kodak with infringing 12 of its instant photography patents.

Thus began the longest and costliest patent battle in U.S. history. When the first phase of the trial was over, some nine years and many tens of millions of dollars later, Judge Rya Zobel of the U.S. District Court in Boston found that Kodak had infringed seven of Polaroid's patents. Her order read: "Kodak, it

also represent the most powerful Grow strategy in your competitive arsenal, especially when IP issues are treated as strategic elements of the R&D process itself. Indeed, a patent-savvy approach to R&D can not only give a company's products a proprietary edge in the marketplace, it can also strongly reinforce the branding and marketing efforts devoted to those products. In short, intellectual property can sometimes be the decisive factor in determining whether a company's R&D program leads to product success or failure, market dominance or share erosion, rising profits or falling margins.

Patents may determine whether your R&D leads to market dominance or erosion.

In this chapter, we show how an effective patent strategy can help R&D managers develop category-leading products and services that dominate markets and create new wealth for shareholders. We expose the patenting myths that continue to cripple R&D effectiveness in so many companies. And we offer a three-pronged approach to patenting—we call it IP-3 for R&D—that helps you select the *right* products to build, bolsters the branding and marketing efforts devoted to them, and guarantees that you and not your competitors control the key methods and processes needed to successfully manufacture, market, and distribute those products to the marketplace.

THE COST OF IP MISMANAGEMENT

Although the Kodak blunder may have been the most expensive example of IP mismanagement in the history of corporate R&D, it is hardly unique. In 1991, Minolta was forced to borrow from its bankers to pay Honeywell $127.5 million after a court ruled it had infringed on the latter's autofocus camera patent—a patent that Minolta may well have thought it safe to infringe because Honeywell was not using it in any products. That same year, the Japanese firm Toyobo was forced to shut down its new drug manufacturing facility after a court ruled it had infringed a Genentech patent for the heart attack drug TPA.[6] More recently, General Electric—the largest company in the world in terms of market capitalization, with over $90 billion in annual revenues— was hauled into court by tiny Fonar Corp. in 1997 for infringing the latter's patented MRI (magnetic resonance imaging) technology, which is used to detect cancers and other diseases in the human body. The result? To its great shock, GE was forced to pay Fonar $128.7 million—an amount equal to ten times the small firm's annual revenues at the time—which Fonar then distributed to its shareholders in the form of "patent infringement" dividends.[7]

Sometimes infringement can cost a company not just its money but its very life. In a patent suit that gives new meaning to the phrase "when the shit hits the fan," diaper maker Paragon Trade Brands was forced into bankruptcy in 1998 by a series of infringement claims. The latest one was settled in January 1999 when Paragon agreed to pay Procter & Gamble $163.5 million up front as well as royalties on all its diaper sales for the next ten years—assuming, that is, that Paragon manages to emerge from Chapter 11.[8] Another case involves the biotech firm Cellpro (see Chapter 1), which was found guilty in 1997 of infringing the patents for human-cell separation technology owned by Johns Hopkins University, Baxter Healthcare, and Becton Dickinson. In this case the judge found Cellpro liable for *willful* infringement and levied treble damages that (along with other claims) ultimately cost the firm $15.6 million. In the end, Cellpro went bankrupt and had to shut down its operations, lay off 93 employees, fire its CEO, and liquidate its assets.[9] Cellpro shares, which had traded as high as $16 prior to the lawsuit, are currently trading at 6¢ per share.

The Costs of Not Patenting

To be sure, infringement is not the only—or even necessarily the greatest—danger confronting companies that ignore intellectual property issues in their R&D efforts. The *failure to patent* the results of innovative research can also lead to huge financial and strategic losses, as illustrated by Xerox's decision in 1979 not to patent its invention of the graphical user interface (GUI) that later formed the basis of Apple's Macintosh and Microsoft's Windows personal computer operating systems. According to Steve Rowe, a researcher at Xerox's Palo Alto Research Center (PARC) at the time and now director of the Product Development consulting practice at PriceWaterhouseCoopers, "All of us at PARC fervently believed in the GUI. But management didn't have a clue what to do with it—they were copier guys, and they didn't see much of a business in what was then a small market for PCs."

A former Xerox patent attorney says Xerox had even gone so far as to write patent applications for some of its GUI technologies, including everything from pull-down menus to pop-up dialog boxes to scalable windows. But at a critical invention disclosure meeting held at the time, it was decided not to proceed with the filings. Clearly, the 1975 FTC consent decree that forced Xerox to license away its copier patents (see Chapter 2) was still inhibiting the firm's patenting practices. But Xerox also seriously underestimated the GUI's significance.

"If we had been really good, we could have [patented it]," admits retiring Xerox CEO Paul Allaire. "We probably should have." [10]

Indeed, even if Xerox had been correct in deciding not to invest the resources to develop and market GUI software at that time—it was, after all, rather far afield from Xerox's traditional lines of business—the company still should have viewed the fruits of its GUI research as corporate assets of potentially great value, if not to itself then to others. Had Xerox patented the GUI, then even at a very conservative royalty rate of 1 percent of sales, the license fees that Xerox might have earned between 1984 and 1998 (when the patent would have expired) from sales of Macintosh and Windows operating system software probably would have topped half a billion dollars.[11] If ever there was an intellectual property "big one" that got away, that nonexistent GUI patent is certainly it.

Xerox wasn't alone in throwing away a possible fortune at the time of the PC's birth. In 1979, a 29-year-old software programmer named Dan Bricklin introduced the first "killer app" of the computer revolution: the spreadsheet program VisiCalc. Spreadsheet programs such as Microsoft Excel and Lotus 1–2–3, used by tens of millions of people today, earn their manufacturers hundreds of millions of dollars. Yet even though Bricklin's spreadsheet was the original from which all others were copied, he did not receive a dime of these riches.

"Alas, a lack of patent protection for VisiCalc plus other business mistakes deprived Bricklin of greater glory—not to mention riches," noted *U.S. News & World Report*.[12]

Perhaps Dan Bricklin can be excused for failing to protect his innovative spreadsheet program, given that computer software was rarely patented in those days. But the Swiss Watchmakers Association had no such excuse when it dismissed as a "mere curiosity" the new electronic quartz watch movement that had been developed by Swiss inventors and presented to the association for patenting. Instead, the Watchmakers Association exhibited the quartz prototype at the next world watch fair, where

Japanese executives and representatives of Texas Instruments realized its potential. In the end, Seiko, Citizen, and other watch companies seized significant market share that Swiss watchmakers have not been able to recover since.[13]

Aside from throwing away corporate assets (as Xerox did) or recklessly inviting the destruction of an entire line of business (as Kodak did), the failure to thoroughly map the patent landscape at an early stage in the R&D process can also lead to a variety of other problems. Product development, branding, and marketing expenditures can be wasted. Litigation costs and the likelihood of expensive patent infringement judgments increase dramatically. Board liability and the threat of shareholder lawsuits are magnified—after all, failing to make best efforts to steer R&D away from potential infringement problems is the intellectual property equivalent of negligently building your factory atop an active seismic fault. And most important of all, the company's ability to intelligently plan its own future by leveraging the innovation within its R&D organization into new growth businesses is seriously compromised.

IP NEGLECT IN R&D IS WIDESPREAD

"Frankly, it's beyond me why any company in this day and age would even attempt to do R&D without the insights that patent mapping gives you," declares Paul Germeraad, the former vice president and director of corporate research at Avery Dennison. "It's like trying to navigate your company's future blind, without a map."

And yet surprisingly, the evidence suggests that this is exactly what the majority of companies in America are attempting to do—navigate blind. Says Germeraad: "From my own experience as a board member of the Industrial Research Institute, I'd guess that not more than a handful of companies in America have a truly deliberate IP strategy driving their R&D."

Indeed, a 1998 survey of 360 companies conducted by the patent information firm Derwent found "major contradictions between the theoretical value that companies place on patents, and their poor management of this vital resource in practice." Although 90 percent of the companies surveyed, for example, agreed that patents could be important to the R&D process—and 54 percent conceded that a patent had "significantly changed their company's fortunes"—an astounding 71 percent neverthe-less admitted that they had wasted R&D expenditure through patent mismanagement. Moreover, although 84 percent of the companies polled claimed to have a patent policy, at least in theory, fewer than half of those (42 percent) ever conducted regular audits to see if that policy was effective or if it was even being implemented.[14]

Another recent study of global intellectual property practices revealed that U.S. companies waste more than one of every three of their patented technologies because they don't appear to have immediate use in product development.[15] Given the rich revenues and exploitable asset values that can often be extracted from such "noncore" patents (a subject that will be discussed in Chapter 5), such neglect is a serious waste of valuable corporate assets. It also ignores the value of strategic patents that, although not used in current products, nonetheless might enable a company to exploit longer-term technology and market trends.

"There is probably no management function in business today that is less understood or less effective than the manage-ment of R&D," declares Paul Turner, the director of R&D effec-tiveness studies for PriceWaterhouseCoopers. "When I ask execu-tives specific questions—What is the process by which your company decides that you're building the right product at the right time? What are the intellectual property factors that went into this decision? And who is ultimately responsible for 'owning' this process within your organization and managing it?—what is amazing to me is that in nine out of ten companies you either get no coherent answers at all or you get very different answers from different people within the organization. All you know is that the process is not really owned, nobody's performance review depends upon it, and it's usually a very suboptimum process in terms of speed or what I call the 'time to decide.'"

Key Factors Inhibiting IP Effectiveness in R&D

How do we account for this apparently widespread neglect of IP management issues in corporate R&D? As noted in Chapter 2, until very recently most firms have tended to treat patents as legal shields rather than strategic business tools. But there are also particular factors that inhibit corporate attention to patent issues in R&D.

Shortened Product Cycles. One factor is the ever-quickening pace of technological change itself. As product life cycles grow ever shorter, the pressure exerted on companies to get to market first becomes greater. So it's hardly a surprise that many R&D managers consider the time and expense needed to patent-protect their products and avoid infringement dangers to be unnecessary. After all, the life span of a new product today is often less than the time required to obtain a patent for it.

In the graphics chip business, for example, design cycles have now reached 18 months in some cases, while product cycles can be as short as 6 months. According to Jon Peddie of the consulting firm Jon Peddie Associates, this creates an "impossible" situation. "With everything moving at Web time now," he asks, "who the hell has time to do a patent search?"[16]

Perhaps a better question to ask is, Who has the time (or the million-plus dollars) it takes to defend against a patent suit? And who can afford to devote a year or more of R&D effort on a product only to have to abandon it later because of an infringement problem that could easily have been spotted and designed around early in the process?

In any event, allowing patenting strategy to be defined solely by the life span of the product itself is a very short-sighted approach. After all, the key enabling technologies in most products usually survive through multiple generations of product revision, as do many of the product's key performance features.

No time for patent analysis? Then how about a patent lawsuit—do you have time for that?

Moreover, these key technologies and performance features are often transferable into new product lines. And because these also usually represent the greatest value-added components of products today, the ignoring of patent issues can leave firms unable to extract the full value of their products' success.

The "Ignorance" Myth. Another factor inhibiting corporate attention to IP issues in R&D is the myth that ignorance is safer—that is, that activities such as patent mapping and analyzing the IP profile of competitors can leave a company open to charges of willful infringement (and the treble damages that can result). Case law, however, makes it clear that mere knowledge of another's patents does not by itself indicate willful infringement; there must be a clear intent to infringe. Yet despite this fact, patent counsels at many firms still advise R&D managers against patent mapping the landscape of competition in their industries.

This probably explains Apple's foolish response to a $1.1 billion patent suit filed by the electronics firm Imatec, which accused Apple of willfully infringing Imatec patents in the development of Apple's ColorSync technology. Apple denied that it infringed Imatec patents, of course, but then went on to argue that it could not possibly have *willfully* infringed them because it "has no policy or procedure for determining, prior to the manufacture or sale of a product, if the product or its method of manufacture infringes a patent owned by another."[17]

In resorting to this "ignorance" defense, however, Apple may have picked up a rock only to drop it on its own feet. For if shareholders can sue companies for mishandling their inventories of widgets, what's to prevent them from coming after boards who mishandle their inventories of patents or who conduct R&D with reckless disregard for potential infringement dangers?

According to Steven Bochner, an attorney at Wilson Sonsini Goodrich and Rosati—a firm that represents more Silicon Valley boards of directors than any other law firm—the prospect of shareholder lawsuits over what he calls "IP wasting" is very real. "[Patent filings] are way up, the amount of patent litigation is increasing, and looking at the class action securities cases, it's foreseeable that at some point a company could be sued if it failed to exercise its duty of care in protecting its IP assets," Bochner asserted.[18]

The prevalence of IP mismanagement in corporate R&D today is lamentable, because intellectual property has become the key strategic resource of the technology-intensive enterprise and it is dangerous in the extreme to waste that resource. Patents, in fact, have become the currency of R&D effectiveness, and that currency can be converted into market-leading products, new growth businesses, a weapon against competitors, increased cash flow and profit, or a future strategic advantage.

What's more, being able to intelligently trade on this IP currency is no longer the time-consuming and expensive process it was just a few years ago. As recently as the mid-1990s, former Avery Dennison R&D chief Paul Germeraad had to plod his way through printed issues of *Patent Gazette* with a yellow highlighter and a razor blade to extract the critical pieces of intellectual property in his field and assemble them into a rudimentary patent map. "It used to take us three to nine months to do a full IP analysis just for one product," Germeraad recalls. "Obviously, we could only do that for one or two of our most critical R&D projects."

But new electronic patent databases, combined with automated data-mining and visualization tools, have reduced the time needed for IP analysis from months to just hours. Given that such tools are becoming affordable even for smaller companies, the question today is not whether a company should integrate patent planning into its R&D effort, but how.

THE IP-3 APPROACH TO CREATING DOMINANT PRODUCTS

There are three key components of any effective patent strategy for developing high-margin, category-leading products:

- *Protect Your Core Technology Advantage:* Use patent mapping to select products that can be buttressed with competitor-blocking patents, then patent the core technologies embodied in these products that deliver the greatest performance advantage over rival products in the market.

- *Reinforce the Product's Differentiating Features:* Reinforce those core patents with a patent wall of IP protection covering the key differentiating features that reinforce and communicate the product's brand positioning and key performance advantages.

- *Control the Process Choke Points:* Patent the key methods and processes—whether these are manufacturing, distribution, or even business methods—that are absolutely essential to the building, marketing, or selling of the product.

Protect the Core Advantage

The first challenge for any R&D organization, of course, is deciding what to build. Certainly the well-run R&D organization will receive systematic input from sales and customer support on what the market wants. Marketing staff will advise R&D on the key features needed to differentiate the product in the market and reinforce its brand distinctiveness. But patent issues should also play a role in shaping product development, both to avoid infringement and to enhance the company's ability to create market-leading products.

Hitachi, which has consistently been among the top ten patenting firms in the world, has a strategic patenting policy that focuses on developing leading products that can command market-dominating or "strategic" patents. "Changes in the market have been occurring very rapidly, so only leading products can generate large profits," explains IP director Ogawa Katsuo. "We are required to select at an early stage the technologies which are likely to lead to leading products, apply for patents worldwide for these technologies, and establish an extensive network of strategic patents so that others will not be able to follow us."

According to Katsuo, leading products are not necessarily the most complex technologically. "Inventions that are very simple are more likely to [yield] strong patents which competitors cannot get around," he explains. By way of example, he cites Hitachi's automotive air flow sensor, which from a technical standpoint would have been easy for competitors to copy.

"We've been able to take a large share of the market," Katsuo explains, "because other companies are aware that we have rigorously protected it with a number of patents and so they didn't pursue us. Had we been careless in our patent application procedures, other companies would have copied this product straight away." Instead, competitors are forced to look for more complex—and therefore more expensive—ways to design around Hitachi's patents, making their air flow sensors less competitive in the market.

Patent issues also strongly influence R&D priorities in the biotechnology and pharmaceutical fields. The biotech firm Genetics Institute, for example, says it decides which version of a drug to develop not only on the basis of which has the best clinical trial results, but also according to which version can command the strongest patent protection. Explains the firm's patent counsel: "The strength of the potential patent position is a leading factor in what research to pursue."[19]

As Alex Brown analyst David G. Webber puts it, "Each patent is like a slat in a stockade. You need to have all the slats in place, so there's no hole."[20]

Probably no consumer product company in America is better at integrating intellectual property management into the R&D process, however, than Gillette. For nearly a hundred years, Gillette has based its market success and brand dominance on its ability to continually invent and then patent new proprietary technologies. The development of Gillette's Sensor shaver a decade ago is an excellent case study in IP-savvy product development.

According to Dr. John Bush, vice president of corporate R&D until his recent retirement, the first challenge in developing the Sensor was to map the patent landscape surrounding the shaver's key performance attribute: its ability, owing to twin independently moving blades, to deliver a closer and more comfortable shave. The technology behind this innovation was called floated angle geometry, and involved mounting tiny springs to twin blades within a cartridge in such a way that each blade could move independently along the contours of a face.[21]

"The engineers had come up with seven different designs for mounting the blades so that they floated," Bush recalls, "and we patented them all." But which of these seven designs should they build the product around? Bush says that the company's patent lawyers worked with R&D from the earliest stages, mapping out the **If you want dominant products, buttress them with dominant patents.** patent territory. And in those days, this was no easy task: patent searching could only be done by going to Washington and examining the patent office database.

Nonetheless, says Bush, "A full patent search was made on all seven versions of the design. This was quite a job as you might imagine, because to determine all the prior art, you had to look at razor patents going all the way back to the last century. But in the end we chose the design that potential competitors would have most difficulty getting around."

The lesson here is that if you want to build dominant products, it helps to pick those that can be buttressed with dominant patents. "Only when R&D activities and patent protection are fully [aligned] can leading products be assured," says Hitachi's Katsuo.

Reinforce the Product's Distinguishing Features

Gillette's patenting of its core floated angle geometry design was only the first of what would become 22 patentable inventions incorporated into the Sensor shaver. The next step was to determine which among the product's key features best communicate the shaver's branded personality and performance advantages to the consumer—and then patent-protect these features. This was an effort that blended engineering, aesthetics, design, marketing, and, of course, patent law.

"We patented the key design features in the cartridge, the springs, the angle of the blades, that sort of thing," explains Bush.

Build a patent wall around your product's key differentiating features.

"There were also patents covering the handle and some of its characteristics. We even patented the container that had the proper masculine sound and feel as it was ripped. We covered all the features that we thought would be of value to the consumer."

In short, says Bush, "We created a patent wall with those 22 patents. And they were all interlocking so that no one could duplicate that product."

The opposite of building a patent wall around your product—or *clustering*, as it is sometimes called—is *bracketing* the patents of your competitors. Perhaps the best way to grasp the concept of bracketing is to imagine that your competitor has invented a new high-intensity light and has patented the filament. But, as it turns out, the filament requires a more durable glass bulb and socket housing to absorb the added heat, as well as more heat-resistant shade construction and electrical connectors. Even new manufacturing processes are required, as is new packaging, for the new-style bulbs can be ruined by the oils from human touch. Your competitor may have patented the filament, but if you patent everything else, then the competitor is locked out of much of the market. That's the essence of bracketing.

Control the Vital Choke-Point Processes

Many companies neglect to protect the vital methods or process choke points that are most essential to successfully manufacturing, marketing, or distributing their new products—even when these are the most critical value-added components of the product.

Wal-Mart is a case in point. The secret of its success is not that it sells better products; it simply sells its products better. Anyone can open a warehouse outlet and stuff it with products, but only Wal-Mart has the sophisticated logistical and marketing systems needed to grow the firm into the largest retailing empire on earth. Unfortunately, Wal-Mart didn't patent this vital choke point in its operation, and so any Wal-Mart employee can (and has) walked out the door with it.

The importance of protecting and leveraging your critical methods and processes cannot be overstated. What if *Wired* had patented its then-pioneering use of click-through banner advertising on the Web in 1994? By licensing it to every other advertising Web site at a nominal 1 percent royalty, the magazine could today be earning an extra $20 million a year. And what if Amazon.com had patented one-click ordering before it became prevalent in on-line shopping? It might now have more than just its brand clout to fend off the onslaught of new rivals like Virgin.

Dell, on the other hand, did secure its process choke points. While the PC vendor has patented some of its product technologies (certain power supply components, for example), the patents covering the manufacturing, distribution, and marketing methods used in its build-to-order direct sales system are truly critical to the PC maker's stunning success.

As for Gillette, the reader will probably not be surprised to learn that it is also rather adept at patenting the methods most critical to its products' success. The key processes involved in manufacturing the floated angle geometry design of the Sensor shaver, for example, were patent mapped and then protected. These included the high-speed photography techniques used in photographing the act of shaving—essential, one would think, to designing better shavers—which were embodied in a device capable of resolving images only one-thousandth of a millimeter that Gillette called the "Whisker Cam."[22] But where the company really excelled in process patenting was in the development of the Sensor's successor, the Mach3 shaver introduced in 1998.

Gillette first patented the Mach3's core technology, of course—a coating process called DLC (Diamond Like Coating) that produced blades ten times thinner and harder than those used in the Sensor (whose innovations were unrelated to the blades themselves). Likewise, the company patented the Mach3's principal design features: the use of three staggered blades, each getting progressively closer to the skin; a new forward pivot design that positions the blades in an optimal shaving position; a rubberized contour grip for better handling; an indicator strip that signals when the shaver is no longer experiencing "the optimal Mach3 shave"; and the "single point" cartridge loading system that makes it impossible to attach Mach3 blades upside down—a problem apparently experienced by 18 percent of shaving men, according to Gillette.[23]

But much of the staggering $750 million spent in the development of the Mach3—and this before the product was even shipped to the stores!—went toward inventing nearly 200 pieces of equipment and technology needed in the manufacturing process. Each of these manufacturing methods was patent mapped and chosen, in part, because Gillette could stake a proprietary claim on it—a process made easier by the placement of new patent servers on the desks of the IP team at Gillette. Among the manufacturing equipment patented is the $20 million vacuum chamber in which the revolutionary DLC blade coating is applied. All told, the Mach3's core technology, key product features, and critical choke-point methods are protected by 35 patents.

Isn't 35 patents for a shaver overkill? On the contrary, says

Bush. Gillette is investing in the new technologies and process innovations it will need to produce the advanced shaving products of the twenty-first century. And it intends to own, rather than rent, those innovations.

ORGANIZING THE IP-3 PROCESS

Each component of the IP-3 for R&D strategy must be conducted at the appropriate phase of the development process, which, at least in large firms, is typically divided into four distinct stages (see Figure 4-1).

Stage 1: Preliminary Assessment

Stage 1 is the *preliminary assessment* phase, during which the R&D team identifies the nature of the product—that is, the market need for it and the target customers who would buy it—and evaluates how the new product and market opportunity fits in with the firm's larger strategic goals. This is when you implement the first element of the IP-3 for R&D strategy: mapping the patent landscape to determine which and how many other competitors may be developing similar products in the field, and whether you can acquire a proprietary position in the market. The publicly available information contained in patent databases will also help you spot potential infringement dangers that need to be avoided. With the assistance of your competitive intelligence, and legal, sales, and marketing staff, you must determine the strength of the patent protection you can obtain for your product concept and then, assuming the analysis is positive, patent the core enabling technologies that deliver the product's key performance advantages over rival products in the marketplace.

FIGURE 4-1   PRODUCT DEVELOPMENT LIFE CYCLE

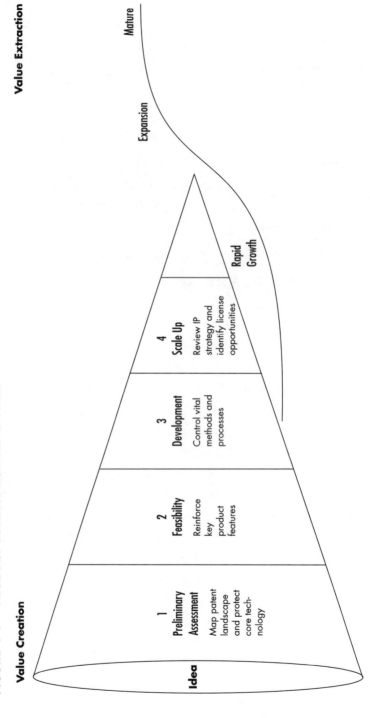

During this first phase of the IP-3 for R&D process, you may discover that others have already patented certain core technologies that you need. If so, then consider licensing those to reduce R&D costs and shorten your time to market.

Figure 4-2, for example, spotlights the patenting profiles of Sony and Intel in the area of MPEG video compression technology. A map such as this could be useful to Sony if, for example, it wished to quickly launch an on-line video gaming venture and was looking for key technology components that it could license in to shorten the time to market. Sony has extensive MPEG experience of its own, of course, but not in MPEG that is optimized for transmission over telephone lines, as Intel appears to have. And luckily for Sony, Figure 4-2 suggests that Intel's MPEG efforts are focused more on the noncompeting arena of

FIGURE 4-2 MPEG PATENT HIT COUNT: INTEL VERSUS SONY

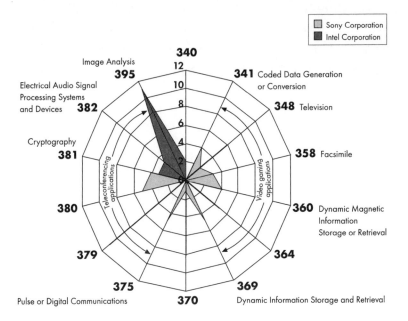

Source: Courtesy of Aurigin Systems, Inc.

teleconferencing rather than on-line gaming. Thus Intel might be open to the idea of licensing its MPEG patents to Sony—and, indeed, might even make an excellent technology and marketing partner.

Stage 2: Feasibility

After Stage 1 has been completed (and assuming the initial assessment is positive), the R&D team moves into the Stage 2 *feasibility* phase. This is when a thorough analysis of the costs, technologies, manufacturing requirements, time to market, and other aspects of the development effort is conducted. The R&D team will also study the patents on similar technologies, both to deepen its understanding of the state of the art and to help the team design around any infringement dangers. But the principal IP task at this stage is to conduct the second of the IP-3 patent tasks—namely, to identify the key features that best differentiate the product in the market and communicate its branded performance advantages, and then build a patent wall around them. With the help of your competitive intelligence, marketing staff, and legal staff, patent analysis may also enable you to uncover the strengths and weaknesses of your competitors' patent positions and develop ways to patent-block or bracket them in the market.

Stage 3: Development

In Stage 3, the *development* phase, the new product is actually developed and prototyped, and the critical manufacturing and other processes are set in place. This is when the third component of the IP-3 for R&D strategy comes into play: patenting the critical manufacturing and other processes that are most essential to the product's successful development and launch in the market. Also at this time, marketing and business development staffers will be formulating the marketing strategy for the product, and patent-mapping work may even be helpful in identifying potential marketing or distribution partners as well.

Stage 4: Scale Up

In Stage 4, the final *scale-up* phase, R&D prepares for the commercial launch of its new product. This is when the rubber of R&D meets the rough road of large-scale manufacturing, quality control, packaging, distribution, and channel development. All previous patenting on the product will be carefully reviewed and revised as needed. Also in Stage 4, initial thought will be given to future line extensions or vertical-market applications of the new product, and the more IP-savvy R&D managers may want to establish initial patent beachheads into these new segments. Patents will also be filed in this stage for noncore technologies or processes that may not be critical to the product at hand but may nonetheless prove valuable down the road either as licensing opportunities, trading chips for technologies you might want to license in, or simply as strategic enabling technologies that strengthen the company's long-term competitive options.

However your company's R&D effort is organized—whether you're a large enterprise running a conventional four-stage R&D effort as outlined here, or a seat-of-the-pants start-up racing to jerry-rig your technologies together at Web speed—patent strategy can be a powerful instrument in your developer's tool kit. It can help you grasp the speed and direction of technology change in your industry. It can reveal the strategies and capabilities of competitors and show you how to beat the patents off them. And it can help you avoid infringement disasters of the type that nearly sank the Eastman Kodak company.

Indeed, by employing the IP-3 for R&D strategy outlined in this chapter, R&D managers can supercharge their ability to create market-dominating products and thus help turn their engineering laboratories into engines of wealth creation for the company and its shareholders.

As Lucent's Executive Vice President of Corporate Strategy, Patricia F. Russo, put it, "We turn ideas into inventions, inventions into patents, and patents into profits."[24]

5

GAINING FINANCIAL LEVERAGE
THROUGH PATENT MINING

Eugene Emmerich—his friends call him "Bill"—is not exactly a household name, though you can be sure that the CEOs of approximately 400 corporations will never forget him. Nor is he one of the darling glitterati of the computer world, despite the fact that if you use any sort of PC at all he is at least partly responsible for what you see on its display screen. But notwithstanding his claim that he's simply "more lucky than smart," the truth of the matter is that Eugene Emmerich is something of an intellectual property wizard.

He is also an inveterate storyteller, and this is one of his favorites. Once upon a time, as Emmerich tells it, a great king was leading his bowmen in battle against a neighboring kingdom. Things were not going well. Suddenly, the king's blacksmith approached, ducking the hail of arrows falling all about. "Great news, sire—we have a new weapon!" he exclaimed, and he held up a machine gun. "Not now!" replied the king. "I've got a war to fight."

Emmerich likes to tell this story to illustrate how, in the heat of daily competitive battle, business leaders often overlook valuable opportunities that, if only seized, could alter the very fortunes of war. Emmerich ought to know. His own company, Cadtrak Corporation, was a flop in the computer-aided design workstation business back in the early 1980s. But by tapping into the revenue streams locked inside Cadtrak's intellectual property portfolio, Emmerich was able to transform a product failure into a patent fortune.

The Cadtrak story begins back in 1980 when the company was formed to develop and manufacture workstations aimed at the architectural, engineering, and construction (AEC) industry. Explains Emmerich, "One of our founders, Josef Sukonick, had patented a means for improving graphics processing. And remember, this was back when processors were slow and memory was very limited. So Joe had come up with the idea of 'selective erase,' which used the logical operator 'exclusive/or' to speed up graphics response time. Anyway, to make a long story short, we had a great technology, a premium group of board members from Bechtel and Fluor, and a wonderful product that, unfortunately, absolutely nobody wanted to buy."

It seems that a recession had hit the industry, and the company was heading straight toward bankruptcy. And there the Cadtrak story might soon have ended, if not for Emmerich's talent for spotting hidden opportunities that others might easily overlook.

"Out of the blue, in 1983, I got this call from the head of licensing at IBM," Emmerich recalls. "He said that they wanted to use our 'selective erase' technology in a couple of their research projects and could we talk about licensing it to them. He really downplayed it as not a big deal. But that started me wondering if maybe there was a business here in licensing our technology, because I was pretty sure that other companies would also want to use it. And sure enough, in 1984 our 'selective erase' technology was written into the EGA graphics specification [and later the VGA specification as well], which meant that basically every computer sold at that time was using our technology. I mean, all you had to do was go to a computer store and look at all the boxes of PCs. If the box said 'EGA compatible,' it had to be using our technology.

"So in 1985," Emmerich continues, "I went to the board and we decided to get out of the workstation business, which was a money loser for us, and concentrate on licensing our patent. And that's what we did. We laid off our 100 employees, and then got to work on licensing."

Emmerich's strategy was simple and effective. "We'd send out a notice to an infringing company's CEO and offer to meet," he explains. "I'd tell him, look, you can always bring in the lawyers later, but let's first try to see if we can work this out without the expense of a suit. I'd tell them they could have as many lawyers and other advisors in the meeting as they wanted, but I'd be coming alone. My coming alone was very important in creating the right atmosphere."

Did any companies refuse to deal? "Oh yes, Commodore [an important computer maker at the time] refused to take a license," Emmerich recalls. "You know, a lot of companies infringe patents; it's really very common. People always try to beat the system. But when you call them on it, and give them a cost-effective way to use your technology legally and avoid the risk of a lawsuit, they usually will. But not Commodore. So we took them to court and got a permanent injunction barring sales of their computers in the U.S. When that happened, their creditors called in their loans and they went bankrupt. That little patent of ours put Commodore out of business."

That "little patent" finally expired in 1997, but not before Emmerich had signed licensing deals with an astonishing 400 companies. "And don't forget," he laughs, "it was just myself and my wife, who managed the business while I was on the road doing licensing deals. Plus we had maybe three secretaries and a couple of PCs between the five of us. And from that, we made something like $50 million. And that's basically all net income, of course."

Five people. Two computers. One patent. That's all it took to make $50 million.

A TRILLION-DOLLAR WAKE-UP CALL FOR CFOs

If a lone wolf like Bill Emmerich could generate $50 million from one patent, it makes you wonder how much more patent gold lies buried within corporate America. We know that patent licensing revenues rose sharply during the 1990s, from $15 billion annually in 1990 to over $100 billion today. But this is probably a drop in the bucket, for we also know that the vast majority of firms today completely ignore the asset value of their intellectual property holdings.

A 1998 survey by the technology transfer firm BTG International, for example, revealed that 67 percent of U.S. companies have technology assets that they fail to exploit. In fact, said the study, American firms on average let over 35 percent of their patented technologies go to waste simply because they have no immediate use in their products. According to the BTG report, the value of these wasted technology assets is at least $115 billion.[1]

That figure is surely too conservative, however, for it assumes that a dollar spent on R&D yields a return of only one dollar. Yet economic data suggest that each dollar a company spends on

R&D increases its market value by as much as $18.70.[2] A recent study on R&D spending in the chemical and pharmaceutical industries, for example, found that $1.00 of R&D produced a return of anywhere from $7.77 to $32.00, depending on the firm. The median return for chemical firms was $15.23 for every dollar spent on R&D; for pharmaceutical companies it was $17.97 for each dollar spent on R&D.[3] Even if we are conservative and assume a cross-industry average return of, say, $10.00 for every dollar spent on R&D, then it would appear that American businesses are ignoring a staggering $1 trillion in intellectual property asset wealth!

THE GREATEST UNTAPPED ASSET OPPORTUNITY

Given the pressures on companies these days to maximize shareholder return by any and all means necessary, the underutilization of this $1 trillion in intellectual property asset values represents either a stinging indictment of executive myopia or the single greatest opportunity to be laid in the lap of corporate chief financial officers in a generation. The CFO's primary duty, after all, is to maximize the utilization of corporate assets no matter their form. And this is

Untapped IP asset values offer CFOs their greatest opportunity in a generation.

precisely what CFOs have been doing for the past decade or so with their structural and human assets—using information technology from SAP, Siebel Systems, PeopleSoft, and other vendors to wring out every dollar of leveragable value they possibly can from their plant and equipment, human resources, and customer support and sales operations.

Now it's time for CFOs to turn their attention to the three-fourths of all corporate wealth that consists of unexploited intellectual assets. For just as the run-up in real estate prices during the 1970s and 1980s resulted in fortunes for the leveraged buy out kings who first saw their potential, the current run-up in intellectual asset values—as evidenced in the growing gap between the book and market values of public companies today—offers enormous opportunities for financial leverage to CFOs (as well as to investors) who are savvy enough to take advantage of them.

In this chapter, we show how CFOs can develop patent strategies that liberate the untapped value of their company's intellectual assets. We explore Grow, Fix, and Sell finance strategies that leverage the hidden value of patent assets to generate new revenue, reduce costs, and enhance corporate financing efforts. And we spotlight some new IP-based investment strategies that CFOs and savvy investors can employ to reduce risk and achieve outsized gains.

USING PATENT "FIX" STRATEGIES TO GENERATE REVENUE

If history is any guide, most companies don't even consider the financial potential of their patent assets until pressed to the wall and struggling to turn around their competitive fortunes. Certainly that was the case with IBM in the early 1990s when, as part of a restructuring effort to reverse its losses and revitalize its strategy, the company began looking for ways to mine its huge patent portfolio. Today, IBM earns a phenomenal $1 billion per year in patent royalties (see Chapter 3). That's one-ninth of its yearly pretax profit!

Notes attorney Victor Siber of the New York law firm Rogers & Wells, "When a company makes a billion on licensing fees, that money goes right to the bottom line. And it's usually money that comes from competitors."[4]

No wonder other firms have been inspired to try replicating Big Blue's licensing success. Lucent is a case in point. Heir to Bell

Labs' impressive patent legacy, Lucent recently centralized all IP assets in a 266-person business unit run along P&L lines. Then, aided by an automated IP management system, Lucent launched a patent licensing program that is already earning several hundred million dollars a year. Vice President of Intellectual Property Michael Greene says his task is to "manage a business whose objective is to make a profit from licensing patents." And with 12 percent of its $30 billion in annual revenues devoted to R&D, notes Vice President of Corporate Strategy Patricia F. Russo, "It's important we get a good return on that investment."[5]

After all, says Lucent IP executive John Peterson, "Once issued, a patent becomes a sunk cost, and can be leveraged or forgotten. To forget is to throw away a potential source of development funding or bottom line contribution. IP should be required to generate returns comparable to other business assets."[6]

A Matter of Life and Death

For some companies, generating revenues from patents can sometimes even be the key to corporate survival. Texas Instruments, for example, was reportedly saved from bankruptcy in the mid-1980s by an all-out patent licensing and litigation effort. In 1992 alone, TI earned $391 million from patent licenses—43 percent more than its $274 million in operating income for that year.[7] Its current licensing revenues are thought to be about $800 million a year. All told, analysts estimate that TI has earned more than $4 billion in royalties since it began enforcing its patents in the mid-1980s. In May 1999, TI signed a licensing pact with Hyundai that is expected to net an additional $1 billion in royalties over the next ten years.

Likewise, National Semiconductor was also saved from bankruptcy in 1990 by an aggressive new patent licensing program under the turnaround regime of Gil Amelio, who later tried to turn Apple Computer around as its CEO in 1997. According to Irving Rappaport, the former vice president and associate general counsel for intellectual property at the firm,[8] patent royalties soared under Amelio's reign to over $200 million between 1991 and 1993.

"I'm not exaggerating when I tell you that National Semiconductor was only weeks away from bankruptcy in late 1990," recalls Rappaport. "All the papers had been filled out and signed before it was decided to continue the business and give licensing a more aggressive push. And without a doubt, patent fees bought us valuable time in which to complete our restructuring process. For a while there, in fact, three-quarters of our revenues came from patent licenses."

To be sure, some firms are simply lucky and stumble upon an accidental gold mine in patent value. A few years ago, attorneys at the Minneapolis law firm of Robins, Kaplan, Miller & Ciresi discovered unused autofocus patents in Honeywell's IP portfolio. They took their information to Honeywell executives, some of whom had no idea the patents even existed and in any event wondered what the big deal was since the company no longer made cameras. The big deal, said the attorneys, was that at least Minolta and probably other companies as well appeared to be infringing Honeywell's patents. In the end, Honeywell earned nearly half a billion dollars in license fees and infringement awards—and in the process forced Minolta to run to its bankers to borrow the $120 million of that amount the courts ordered it to pay.[9]

Xerox: The Next IBM of Patent Licensing?

As we discussed in Chapter 3, Xerox is currently in the midst of a major restructuring and IP revitalization effort under the leadership of new CEO Rick Thoman, who, as the former chief financial officer at IBM, knows full well the contributions that patent licensing can make to a firm's balance sheet. With the formation of Xerox Intellectual Property Operations (XIPO), formerly called the Intellectual Capital Business Unit (ICBU), the company reportedly intends to grow its license revenues from the $8.5 million earned in 1997—a

Companies must look at IP *offensively* and start treating it as a moneymaker.

paltry figure insufficient even to cover the maintenance and tax costs on the portfolio—to $180 million by the year 2002. Don't be surprised, however, if their royalties are easily double that amount.

"[XIPO's] role is to look at the total portfolio of patents and technology and figure out how best to package, market and sell them as we would any other product," explained the late general patent counsel Barry Smith.[10] Patent lawyers such as himself, he added, have a new job: instead of just *protecting* intellectual property, they have to look at IP *offensively* and start treating it as a moneymaker.

One technique that Xerox may employ in its licensing effort is to identify groups of patents within its portfolio that could be licensed together as a package. This can be done by analyzing co-citation clustering patterns. That is, if other firms consistently cite a cluster of Xerox patents in their own, then it may be advantageous for XIPO to package those patents and market them as a group. The marketing of technology assets was previously unheard of at Xerox.

"What was missing before, and what we're now doing, is a systematic mining of our patent portfolio for opportunities," explains Vice President of Intellectual Property Jan Jaferian. "This means, first and foremost, waging a proactive and aggressive effort to generate revenue from our patents. But it also means looking for other uses for our technology besides in products or just sitting on the shelf. If you only use your patents to protect your products, which is the old paradigm, you're missing all manner of revenue-generating and other opportunities."

XIPO's effort marks a radical departure in how the company has historically looked at its intellectual property. "People here used to be too concerned about the cost of filing and maintaining patents," explains CEO Thoman. "They tended to view patent filings as an expense rather than a revenue opportunity. Also, the notion of suing people to protect your intellectual property rights was something that just wasn't done here. Xerox was very much a white glove company—it didn't go for the bare-knuckles, down in the dirt kind of action. One of our people told me that he wanted to sue infringers some years ago and was told that Xerox didn't do that sort of thing."

But those days are over, insists Thoman, who argues that the effort against infringers is important for several reasons. Winning a few infringement suits, he says, will establish Xerox's credibility as a company that no longer wastes its technology or allows others to use it without appropriate compensation. And then, of course, there's the potential contribution to the bottom line from licensing. "We're just starting the process of suing people," he explains. "We'll win one or two of these cases and the money will be big, and then everyone will start to pay up." The company's highest-profile infringement action to date is a lawsuit against archrival Hewlett-Packard for allegedly violating some of Xerox's color inkjet patents.

To help detect infringement, the company has set up a "break-down" lab to examine other companies' products for possible infringement of Xerox patents. "As we've started to do these tear-downs, we're finding some extremely interesting things," explains Thoman. "We believe, for example, that the intellectual content of the Palm Pilot [made by 3Com] is ours. And we think one of the big Japanese companies will be owing us money. It seems that every time we pick up a rock there's money underneath it. It's a nice problem to have."

Patent Analysis to Spot Infringement

In conjunction with the efforts of a product break-down lab, patent analysis can also help to spot potential infringers. Figure 5-1, for example, shows a Patent Citation Tree that indicates that a host of firms, from Ford to Baxter International to archrival Hewlett-Packard, have all cited one fundamental Xerox inkjet patent. By drilling down to their individual patents (not shown), we discover they are using inkjet-like technology in applications as diverse as the spraying of particulate matter onto silicon surfaces, the making of circuit boards, and the fabricating of silicon microstructures.

Whether any of these firms are infringing the Xerox patent we cannot say. It's worth noting, however, that the more often a patent is cited—and this Xerox patent is cited an incredible 2,168 times—the more fundamental it is and therefore the harder to get around without infringing. Furthermore, whenever a company cites a number of your patents, the likelihood of infringement increases. Finally, the further afield from your original application a firm's use of similar technology is, the more likely it is infringing—or the more likely it is that the firm is a good licensing prospect or joint venture partner.

CREATING WEALTH THROUGH IP-BASED "GROW" STRATEGIES

As noted earlier, Grow strategies typically deal with exploiting new markets and new business opportunities over an 18-month

FIGURE 5-1   XEROX PATENT CITATION TREE

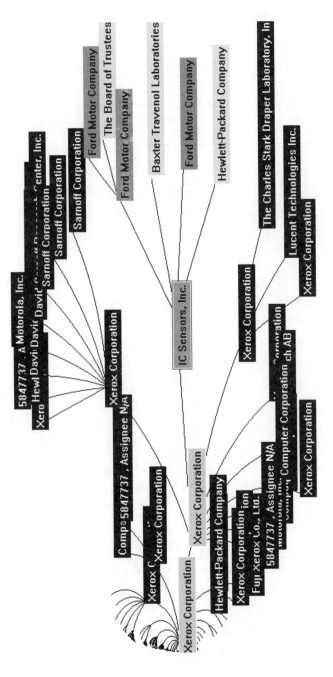

Source: Courtesy of Aurigin Systems, Inc.

to 5-year time frame. Most patent-based financial strategies are of the Fix variety and are aimed at boosting incremental revenue, like those described in the previous section. But sometimes the financial upside of tapping a patent portfolio's value is so great as to constitute a major business in its own right.

Walker Digital, for example, is an intellectual property laboratory modeled after Thomas Edison's famous Menlo Park, New Jersey inventors' lab. In exchange for giving its first spin-off company, Priceline.com, the rights to its e-commerce business model patents, Walker Digital received 7.5 million Priceline shares. One year later, Walker Digital's Priceline shares were worth a phenomenal $1 *billion.*

Then there's the case of SGS-Thomson (now STMicroelectronics), which believed it saw a hidden revenue growth opportunity in the unexploited patent portfolio of chip maker Mostek, owned by United Technologies. It bought Mostek in 1985 for $71 million, and by 1992 had squeezed out over $450 million in licensing revenues.[11] Wouldn't you like to be the CFO that brought the Mostek opportunity before the board of SGS-Thomson?

Utilizing Other People's Patents

Some creative enterprises have even found ways to maximize the asset value of *other* companies' patents. Boston's Sepracor, for example, has developed a unique approach that leverages drug companies' life-and-death dependence on patents into a very valuable business. Sepracor looks for blockbuster drugs that are nearing patent expiration, then improves them by cleaning out unwanted molecules. The firm then obtains a patent on its modified drug and sells the patent back to the original drug manufacturer. In early 1999, Sepracor received $90 million in up-front fees plus future royalties from Eli Lilly, which bought its patent for an improved version of the hit drug Prozac, which had been due to go off patent in a couple of years. The deal is good for Lilly as well, because for every additional year that Prozac remains on patent, Lilly earns an extra $1 billion. And Lilly is not the only prospective Sepracor customer. It is estimated that drugs with annual sales of more than $12 billion are slated to lose their patent protection by the year 2001.

So rich is the exploitable asset potential of intellectual property, in fact, that some firms have made patents their sole product and raison d'être. BTG and InterDigital, for example, are just two of several intellectual property–based businesses that are engaged in the buying, development, and licensing of technology patents. According to the *Wall Street Journal,* BTG executives like to refer to themselves as "merchant scientists" who roam the world "prowling for great ideas to license to deep-pocketed manufacturers." [12] The company splits license revenues 50-50 with the patents' original inventors, and currently holds over 8,500 patents involving some 300 different technologies, including the basic cholesterol test done through blood samples. Its stock, reports the *Journal,* was one of the top-performing issues in Britain in 1998. InterDigital's focus is on the development and licensing of wireless communications patents. Between January 1998 and June 1999, the company earned more than $140 million from licensing. Another intellectual property licensing firm is University Technologies, which also uses its patents to spin off new ventures.

"Historically, licensing has provided our cash flow," explains University Technologies CEO Oleh Hnatiuk, who has led the creation of 13 new companies out of the firm's patents. "You want to maximize the commercial benefits of technology, and if you restrict yourself to licensing, you might not be able to do that." [13]

"SELL" STRATEGIES THAT TURN LOSERS INTO WINNERS

The asset value of patents can also be leveraged for financial gain through a variety of Sell strategies, which companies typically employ when they want to relieve themselves of poorly performing or nonstrategic businesses in the most profitable way possible.

Consider the April 1999 sale by Eastman Kodak of its copier business to the German printing company Heidelberger. For Kodak, says Goldman Sachs analyst Jack Kelly, "The deal means getting rid of a small per-share loss." In exchange for the transfer of its copier patents to a joint venture with Heidelberger, Kodak received $100 million in cash.

This is not the first time that Kodak has employed a patent-based Sell strategy. In 1994, the company also divested its chemical unit (now Eastman Chemical),

A patent strategy can help Wall Street see a company's true competitive prospects and earnings potential.

but in that case the motive was altogether different. According to Eastman Chemical's general counsel Harry Gwinnell, the divestiture was spurred in part by "the inability of the company to educate Wall Street as to the true nature of the business and its earning potential"—including the earning potential and asset value of its extensive portfolio of chemical product and process patents.

In the case of the Digital Equipment Company, patents appear to have been a key component of its strategy of preparing the firm for sale. In 1997, DEC was able to unload its hemorrhaging Alpha chip manufacturing operations to Intel—and receive a sum reported to be $1.5 billion from Intel in return—by agreeing to drop its patent infringement suit against the giant chip maker. Shortly afterward, Compaq Computer bought DEC for nearly $8 billion.

Finally, IP-based Sell strategies can also help a company reduce its costs. In 1999, for example, Dupont donated 23 of its unused patents to universities and nonprofit groups. As a result, instead of having to pay the maintenance costs of keeping them in its portfolio, Dupont received a $64 million tax write-off. A similar donation recently netted Dow a $4 million write-off.

From Bankruptcy to $400 Million?

Perhaps the highest-stakes financial Sell strategy using patents involves the bankruptcy of the supercomputer company Thinking Machines Corporation. Back in the 1980s, Thinking Machines had pioneered a new approach to supercomputing called "massively parallel processing" and invested $150 million developing and patenting new technologies relating, among other things, to the way processors communicate with each other and access data in memory and storage. By the early 1990s, however, the vagaries of the market—not to mention a less-than-adept management team, say insiders—forced the firm to seek reorganization under Chapter 11 bankruptcy proceedings.

There the story might have ended—and along with it, some 200 patented technologies—had not key executives pulled together a group of creditors, shareholder representatives, and intellectual property experts to try to recoup the value of all that innovation and investment. Their plan? Sever Thinking Machines' intellectual property rights from the defunct operating company and create a new, separate holding company whose sole purpose was to exploit these patents through licensing and, if necessary, litigation.

According to Mark Lieberman, the founding chairman of the new holding firm TM Patents, having a completely separate patent holding structure offered a significant advantage. "Look at it this way," Lieberman explains. "Suppose you're a small company, and you've got this nice little portfolio of 200 valuable patents. What happens when you go and knock on the door of some large corporation and you tell them that they're infringing on your patents so they had better take out a license?"

What happens, of course, is that the large corporation informs you that their lawyers are bigger than your lawyers—so go take a hike. "Exactly," says Lieberman. "Or they'll tell you that if you're smart, you'll just cross-license with them and walk away while you still can. Because otherwise they're going to litigate you so far into the next millennium you'll wish you never even heard of the word 'patent.'"

But because TM Patents is a holding company with no products, no operations, and no sales, says Lieberman, it can't be sued. "That's the key: no exposure," he explains. "While we can sue for infringement, we can't be countersued because we're not making or selling any products, so there's no way we could possibly be infringing anyone else's patents. Our only 'product,' if you will, is intellectual property."

An engineer and patent lawyer by training, Lieberman served as Assistant Secretary for Technology and then Associate Deputy Secretary of the U.S. Department of Commerce before returning to private business, where in addition to his continuing role as a part-time director of TM Patents, he is now top executive at an Internet company. TM Patents' current chairman is A. Sidney Alpert, former head of the IP licensing firm University Patents (since renamed Competitive Technologies) and now vice president and general counsel of California-based start-up 3D Systems.

According to Alpert, an authority on patent valuations who frequently serves as an expert witness in patent litigations, TM Patents' holdings could net several hundred million dollars over the next five years—and that's just from its data access and storage patents. The firm has additional patents covering super-computing and other technologies as well.

VALUATION TOOLS FOR IP ASSET EXPLOITATION

Before a company can take advantage of a Grow, Fix, or Sell strategy aimed at maximizing its intellectual asset values, let alone make use of the value of patents as financing and investment vehicles, the CFO must attempt to get a rough idea of what those values are. Unfortunately, this is no easy task. For one thing, valuation methods for intangible assets such as intellectual property are at best rudimentary, and the subject of more than a little debate and controversy. For another, markets for the trading of patent assets are still in their infancy and thus of little help in providing reliable valuation benchmarks. Such markets include the proposed Virtual Components Exchange (VCE), which the *Wall Street Journal* says intends to become a "shopping mall for chip intellectual property," and the Patent & License Exchange (PLX), slated to launch on the Internet in late 1999. Nonetheless, it is possible to obtain at least a rough valuation of your IP assets, and a number of consulting firms exist that can help you do so. But as we noted in Chapter 3, the valuation effort begins with an audit that separates your patents into core and noncore groups.

Core patents cover technologies that are or will be embodied in current or future products. These have very little in the way of market-based guidelines for valuation since they are usually (but not always) not the subject of licensing efforts. Instead, their value lies mainly as enablers of the commercial opportunities being pursued by the business units whose products contain the patented technologies. In its valuation efforts, for example, Dow

Chemical uses a tool called the "Tech Factor Method" invented by Arthur D. Little consultants that quantifies the monetary contribution of each patent as a percentage of the business's total net present value. Alternatively, a RAND Corporation study sets the value of a patent as being equivalent to an R&D cash subsidy rate of up to 25 percent.[14]

Noncore patents, on the other hand, cover technologies that are not being used in either current or planned products. Because such patents can be the focus of IP licensing efforts, they are sometimes easier to value. Licensing rates vary from industry to industry, but usually range between 1 and 5 percent of the gross sales of products or services that employ a patented technology. Another approach, the "25 percent rule," sets royalties as a percentage of net profits. Many companies choose to outsource their licensing programs to independent firms with more experience in the field, at a cost of somewhere around one-third of royalties earned. It's worth noting, by the way, that intellectual property analysis tools can help in the valuation effort of both core and noncore patents. A number of studies have shown that the more often a company's patents are cited by those of other firms, the more important is the technology—and, therefore, the more valuable is the patent.

Proxy Methods of IP Valuation

Rather than attempting to divine the value of each individual patent, however, many firms simply assign some portion of their total market capitalization as a proxy for the value of their intellectual property. The easiest of these proxy methods is simply to subtract the firm's book value from its market value. What remains is then considered the value of its knowledge assets.

There are several limitations to this approach, however. It assumes that book assets have no value above their reported cost. Furthermore, since this measure is subject to the daily vicissitudes of the stock market, the values assigned to intellectual property will tend to fluctuate in a manner not necessarily related to the real underlying value of the IP assets themselves.

NCI Research (affiliated with Northwestern University's Kellogg School of Business) gets around this problem by employing performance-based measurements. NCI suggests that you multiply the average return on tangible assets (ROA) for your industry by your firm's tangible assets, then subtract that number from your pretax earnings and multiply this "excess return" by your three-year average income tax rate, subtracting the result from your "excess return" to arrive at the after-tax premium attributable to your intangible assets. Finally, calculate the net present value of this after-tax premium over the remaining economic life of your patents, dividing it by an appropriate discount rate, such as your cost of capital. What you are left with is the calculated intangible value (CIV) of your intangibles, including your IP.[15]

An alternative approach is offered by Baruch Lev, the Philip Bardes Professor of Finance and Accounting at New York University's Leonard Stern School of Business. Lev's Knowledge Capital Scorecard employs standard after-tax return yardsticks to drive the analysis. Subtract from the firm's annual normalized earnings the earnings from tangible and financial assets (which you get by multiplying the recorded assets by their respective after-tax expected returns—for example, 7 percent for tangible assets and 4.5 percent for financial assets). The remainder represents the earnings generated by knowledge assets. Divide this by the knowledge capital discount rate—that is, the expected rate of return for knowledge assets (which for the software, biotech, and pharmaceutical industries, at least, is 10.5 percent). The result is the value of your IP assets.

PATENT-BACKED FINANCING STRATEGIES FOR BUSINESS

With at least a rough approximation of the value of your intellectual assets in hand, you are ready to consider various means of tapping their value either for financing or investment purposes. *Forbes* magazine, not known for wild-eyed financial speculation, believes that underutilized patent values offer some exciting new possibilities for firms:

> *Here is a way for corporations to generate cash, bundle patents and patent portfolios into investment grade instruments [and] identify forgotten or underutilized patents with economic potential. Just as corporate divisions can sell minority stakes to partners, there is no reason patent portfolios couldn't be treated in exactly the same manner.*[16]

Securitizing Patents for Cash

One of the most intriguing of the new patent-backed financing strategies being discussed is securitization. The idea is explained by Ethan Penner, the legendary Nomura financier who revolutionized the mortgage business in the early 1990s by pooling securitized loans into diversified portfolios and selling them to institutional investors.

"Any predictable income stream, whether from mortgage loans backed by tangible assets such as homes or royalty revenues backed by intangible assets such as intellectual property, can be securitized," argues Penner.

Intangibles already represent a small but growing segment of the $200 billion a year business in asset-backed securities. Following Prudential Securities' successful issuance of $55 million worth of bonds backed by the future royalties from rock star David Bowie's records in 1997, Nomura Asset Capital Corp., Bear

Stearns, and other financial industry heavyweights have also gotten into the business of securitizing entertainment-industry
intellectual property. These loans will be pooled into diversified
portfolios and sold to institutional investors. Many on Wall Street
believe this new form of financing may alle-

Intellectual property represents a new vehicle for financing and investment.

viate the historic mismatch between the industry's high up-front development costs
and the anticipated cash flows from future
earnings that are received only incrementally
over time.

Could not the same approach be taken
with patent portfolios? "Absolutely," insists Penner. "It doesn't
have to be mortgages or even entertainment properties. It could
be credit card receivables. Health care insurance premiums. Or
patent royalties."

The benefits of patent securitization go beyond the financing
derived. "Some of these companies may have a lot of debt,"
Penner explains, "and this naturally affects both their balance
sheets as well as their stock prices. But with securitization, now
these companies have a way to borrow against their patent
portfolios and, what's more, do it off balance sheet. That's
because these loans would be non-recourse and secured only by
the patents."

Although patent securitization is unlikely to become widespread until risk factors can be more easily quantified—and
despite the emergence of various patent infringement insurance
schemes, this will probably not happen anytime soon—some
pioneering securitization efforts have already gotten under way.
In January 1999, the San Francisco–based investment banking
boutique Global Asset Capital announced the first-ever securitization of patent assets—in this case, the estimated future royalties of a cancer drug patent will be securitized and sold to investors.[17] Two months later, the first-ever conference on intellectual

property asset securitization was held in New York City, with presentations from some of the leading investment banking firms in the United States. According to the conference agenda, "Securitizing and valuing intellectual property are the hottest balance-sheet topics in the marketplace."

Leveraging Patents for Small Business Financing

The benefits of IP-based financing are not just reserved for large firms, however. The value of a small start-up company's patents can enhance its efforts to secure financing. Indeed, a strong IP portfolio is sometimes even a precondition of funding.

A patent attorney at Sun Microsystems, for example, insists that some venture capitalists "won't even talk to a start up" nowadays unless it has patents on its ideas.[18] Adds Richard Brandt, editor of Silicon Valley business magazine *Upside*, "VCs still seem hung up on 'barriers to entry.' They like patents. Patent your software, or whatever you plan on selling."[19]

And it's not just barriers to entry that venture investors are seeking when they put money into a patent-holding start-up company. "Intellectual property also creates the ability to get better margins," insists investment banker Michael Kann. "And it creates expansion capacity—the ability to [more effectively] grow your business."[20]

To be sure, strong patents—and a strong patent strategy— merely augment rather than guarantee a firm's competitive prospects. "Yes, patents can be important in our decision to invest in a company," notes Peter C. Wendell, founder and general partner of Silicon Valley–based Sierra Ventures, which has invested over $400 million in information technology and health care start-ups. "But I would not say that they are a singularly sufficient reason to get us or any other venture firm to part with their money. The key factors for success in an entrepreneurial situation still generally go back to management rather than technology."

Battery Ventures' Bob Barrett has no dispute with that view. But he insists that venture investors are starting to pay more attention to the IP strength of prospective start-up investments. "Intellectual property assets are the most underutilized type of corporate asset," he points out. "Yet they offer tremendous leverage for creating and maintaining shareholder value."

Even the conservative banking community is waking up to the value of patent assets. Small businessman Howard Brand believes that his intellectual property portfolio was a critical factor in obtaining a bank loan for his southern California business. "We raised $13 million in financing altogether, and $5 million of the total [was based] on the strength of the intellectual property," he says. "Investors have known the value of intellectual property for a long time; now bankers also realize that they can put numbers not just on hard assets but on the value of intangibles like patents and brand names."[21]

Adds David Blaine, chairman of the Mentor Group, an investment banking firm, "A professional evaluation can be very useful for the entrepreneur seeking startup capital because it gives the investor an independent estimation of the dollar value of the [firm's technology]."[22]

Patent Strategies for Investors

If patents can sometimes assist a company in achieving its financing goals, they are also becoming important in investor relations. Indeed, Wall Street is becoming cognizant of the asset value of patents, and by developing a strategy for leveraging their value, a CFO can better communicate the firm's total asset picture and earnings prospects to the investment community. "The [IP] capabilities of companies are becoming one of the indicators that stock analysts look at as they evaluate the potential of a company," notes Kathy Harris, a research director at the Gartner Group.[23] Investors, too, are becoming more savvy about the role that patents play in corporate valuations. After a judge dismissed a patent suit against laser maker Visx on June 4, 1999, its shares jumped 31 percent in one day.

Investor newsletters that examine corporate performance through the lens of intellectual property have also begun to appear. In the first issue of the *Intellectual Capital Monitor: Patents and Performance,* articles such as "Patents in the Semiconductor Industry: Who Will Come Out Ahead When the Slump Is Over?" and "Rambus' Unique Patent Strategy Creates Value for Shareholders" analyzed the comparative advantage of firms based on their patent strength and offered insights not usually seen in traditional stock analysis.[24]

Then there's noted stock analyst Michael Murphy's new Technology Investing service, which evaluates investment opportunities in the biotech sector by asking this question: Whose patents will create wealth for investors? To judge from Murphy's stock picks, he appears to have been successful in getting his readers into profitable situations ahead of the crowd: Immunex (187.2 percent profit), Premisys (146.2 percent), Genentech (521.1 percent), and IDEC (375 percent).

Fund manager James Oelschlager of the White Oak Growth Stock Fund says he also uses patents "as a measure of productivity" in his analysis—and to good effect, apparently, for the fund has beaten the market with a five-year 32 percent annualized return. Oelschlager believes today's economic climate and rapid technological changes bear similarities to the rapid-growth phase of the Industrial Revolution. "I think we're going through that kind of thing now," Oelschlager argues. "Patents accelerated then, and patents are accelerating now. Many [investors] missed the first industrial revolution, and I think many will miss this one, too."

New York University's Baruch Lev agrees: "Hardly any financial analyst on Wall Street takes patents into account when they study a company, [but] if they knew about the correlation between patents and profits, they might change their approach."[25] Professor Lev and doctoral student Zhen Deng recently studied the stock performance of hundreds of companies over a ten-year period, in fact, and found that companies with more frequently cited (and therefore more valuable) patents saw their stock prices rise far more rapidly than those of other firms.

What does the future hold for IP-savvy investors? A few private investment syndicates have already invested in undervalued patent assets. But *Forbes* magazine speculates that with the value of intellectual property rising by leaps and bounds in the burgeoning knowledge economy, the packaging of patent rights into investment instruments may become more commonplace. "Investors can identify promising patents, owned by individual inventors, or even promising patent portfolios currently under license by companies." And what's more, notes *Forbes*, "The payoff for an investor group could be every bit as great as for a venture capital investment—and there are many fewer people chasing the deals."

All that's needed, says the magazine, is for "a Michael Milken to arise in the world of intellectual property."[26]

Whether the "Michael Milken of IP" will be an individual investor or a corporate CFO, two things are already clear.

First, the huge IP asset values lying untapped in intellectual property portfolios offer the greatest financial opportunity since the leveraged buyout mania of the 1980s.

And second, the greatest gains will go to those who get to the IP asset feast first.

6

PATENT MAPPING YOUR BUSINESS
DEVELOPMENT STRATEGY

Imagine, if you will, that you are the founder of a company whose technology could dramatically speed up Internet communications to millions of homes and offices. Several successive management teams have failed to build the business as hoped, however, and now you've run out of money. Rather than try to secure yet another round of financing and a new executive team, you decide to sell your firm to a major corporation that has the management expertise, financial resources, and marketing muscle needed to push the business forward.

Several problems stand in the way of any acquisition, however. For one thing, you've lost $30 million in the last year on barely $13 million in sales, and frankly, your near-term earnings prospects lie somewhere between "negligible" and "Night of the Living Dead." Even worse, your CEO and management team are dead set against a buyout and have refused to cooperate with prospective buyers. And if all that isn't enough, you also have one of the world's largest telecommunications companies, AT&T, actively conspiring to destroy you.

So, how much do you think you can fetch for your firm in an acquisition—assuming, of course, that you can get a potential buyer to stop laughing long enough to make an offer?

Would you guess $26 million, or two times sales? Or should you really be bold here, discounting your earnings deficiency and management troubles while placing a premium on the fact that your technology serves the fast-growing Internet marketplace, and attempt to value the company as high as ten times revenues, or $130 million?

Try $395 million. Texas Instruments paid a staggering 30 times sales in November 1997 to acquire tiny Amati Communications, a pioneer in Digital Subscriber Line (DSL) technology that greatly speeds data communications over telephone lines.

What could possibly have possessed the semiconductor giant to pay so much for a money-losing firm like Amati? The industry trade weekly *Interactive Week* hinted at the answer:

> *Texas Instruments, Inc. last week turned the high-speed communications equipment industry upside down and gave it a good shake. With a surprising bid of $395 million to acquire Amati Communications, holder of key patents used in the North American standard version of Digital Subscriber Line, TI not only announced its major entry into what it sees as a $6 billion digital modem market, but also took that industry in a new direction.*[1]

"*Amati . . . holder of key patents*"—was that the reason? Amati founder John Cioffi, a Stanford University engineering professor who took a sabbatical in 1991 to start the company, confirms that indeed it was: "It was the intellectual property, absolutely. That, and the fact that TI was really behind in next-generation modem technology and acquiring us was a way to throw themselves in the lead very quickly. These were very strong patents, 25 in all, including those pending. And they had already been adopted by the American National Standards Institute [and later by international standards bodies] as the standard for DSL."

In buying Amati's patents, TI gained more than simply exclusive rights to the technology. According to Gary Seamans, CEO of Westell Technologies, which also bid for Amati but lost to TI's higher all-cash offer, "One advantage of owning intellectual property, as Amati does, is that you are in a position to develop very favorable partnership and licensing relationships."[2]

Another motivating factor was TI's need to keep costs down in a market that will require the delivery of high-speed DSL modems to consumers at affordable prices. As Daniel Briere, president of the consulting firm TeleChoice, observes, "In a commodity market, low cost wins, and the lowest cost players are usually those who own the intellectual property."[3]

Still, as noted earlier, the Amati acquisition faced hurdles that probably would have sunk any other deal. "It would be hard work for a large conservative company like TI to absorb a Silicon Valley start-up anyway, but in our case it was even worse," Cioffi concedes. "Our CEO and management team were steadfastly against the sale, so it basically had to be done over their dead bodies, which obviously made things difficult. And then we had the problems with AT&T. They had a competing technology, but the [standards groups] picked ours instead. So they spent millions of dollars trying to reverse the decision. And we were losing sales because of that."

In the end, however, Cioffi's sale of Amati to TI went ahead successfully—a testament, in large part, to the value of its patents and the engineering team that created them. Today, John Cioffi is back teaching at Stanford—"a lot better off financially than I was before," he acknowledges—and the several professor friends of his who lent Amati money when it was on the ropes have received a hefty return on the faith they showed in the company. And what about AT&T? "Now they're one of the users of our technology," notes Cioffi with a chuckle.

IP's NEW ROLE FOR MERGERS AND ACQUISITIONS

Welcome to the new world of mergers and acquisitions, in which intellectual property has joined such traditional M&A motivators as scale economics and market-share growth to become a key driver of corporate combinations. To be sure, patent-driven mergers, acquisitions, and divestitures have largely been confined to the more hotly contested, technology-intensive sectors of the economy. But as the pace of technology change quickens—and the search for competitive advantage in today's cutthroat global economy becomes ever more desperate—intellectual property is certain to play an increasingly important role in shaping M&A activity throughout all sectors of the economy.

As most readers are well aware, M&A activity has been running at a fever pitch in recent years, and shows no signs of letting up. Indeed, given the surge of deal-making now sweeping the Internet, 1999 may even top 1998's record $2.5 trillion in deals.

Patent mapping can uncover M&A opportunities and strengthen due diligence efforts.

Driven both by the desire of traditional off-line businesses to find on-line partners and by the consolidation and shakeout pressures beginning to batter the developing e-commerce sector, Net mergers increased 22-fold in recent months and are now almost a daily event.

"On the Internet, you have to get bigger fast," says Mark Shafir, head of Merrill Lynch's technology merger practice. "It's going to be the land of the titans pretty quickly."[4]

Despite the mania for mergers, however, it seems that few corporate marriages actually deliver the results desired. A recent study by A.T. Kearney indicates that 58 percent of the 115 multi-billion-dollar mergers that the firm studied did not produce any extra benefit for their shareholders compared with the average for companies in the same industry. What's more, 62 percent of firms failed to outperform their peers in profit growth after the mergers, and 75 percent were unable to meet the strategic goals that motivated the mergers in the first place.[5] Another study by McKinsey & Company found that only 23 percent of the 116 major deals it studied earned back their cost of capital.[6]

In the face of such frenzied (if not especially fruitful) deal-making, business development professionals face difficult challenges. How can they find more attractive M&A opportunities? Are there better valuation and due diligence methods that would reduce the risks involved? And how can such deals be structured to better advantage? Much is at stake in the answers to these questions, for no other corporate action is so public a demonstration of a company's true strategy and vision—or as revealing to competitors, partners, and investors of its genuine strengths and weaknesses—as the mergers and acquisitions decisions a company makes.

In this chapter, we show how business development executives can develop patent-savvy Grow, Fix, and Sell strategies that significantly enhance M&A effectiveness. Whether your company's goal is to acquire an emerging new technology or gain patent-protected entry into a lucrative new market, you'll discover in this chapter how to use patent-based competitive intelligence tools to help uncover the most attractive M&A opportunities, greatly improve valuation and due diligence efforts, and configure M&As and divestitures to take maximum advantage of the many tax, legal, and competitive advantages that are available to IP asset sales.

PATENT-SAVVY M&A "GROW" STRATEGIES

One of the most important advantages of a patent-savvy M&A Grow strategy is that it enables companies to respond quickly to shifts in the technological landscape by seizing the high ground—namely, the key patent portfolios. This is precisely what Texas Instruments did when, realizing that growing demand for higher-speed Net communications made DSL a leading technology for next-generation modems, it moved swiftly to acquire Amati's patent portfolio.

The same motive undoubtedly lay behind Microsoft's 1997 purchase of WebTV Networks, a then-struggling start-up offering Internet service over TV, for $425 million. It was no secret that Microsoft was interested in the huge TV-watching market; indeed, Microsoft would later invest over $7 billion in a number of deals with cable TV and other companies targeting the TV-viewing audience. But why, analysts wondered, would Gates pay so dearly for a firm that was hemorrhaging red ink and had attracted, at that time, fewer than 60,000 customers? After all, Microsoft's $7,000 cost per subscriber in the acquisition was nearly 4 times the cable industry average, and a whopping 40 times the Internet industry average. The press and most analysts were at a loss to explain the economic logic behind the WebTV deal, but the answer to the mystery was really quite simple: when TVs began to look like viable Internet access devices for PC-challenged consumers, Microsoft moved quickly to lock up WebTV's 35 seminal patents covering the delivery of Internet content over TV.

The desire to lock up an emerging new market technology also probably lay behind Microsoft's purchase a year later of Firefly Network, a bankrupt developer of "collaborative filtering" software that facilitates customization of Web content according to Net users' interests. The price paid was $40 million in stock, cash, and assumed debt. Analyst Geoffrey Bock of the Patricia Seybold Group noted, "I think Microsoft is buying intellectual property—I would assume there's a patent pending on this—and they're also buying some very skilled tech talent."[7]

Gaining Patent-Protected Entry into New Markets

Acquiring the rights to emerging market-leading technologies is only one way that IP-driven mergers can serve a company's growth strategy, however. They can also help companies gain patent-protected entry into hotly contested new markets.

Consider, for example, the Machiavellian M&A maneuverings over patent rights in the stent medical device business. Stents are tiny wire mesh devices that keep a coronary artery open after it has been cleaned out by an angioplasty procedure, and until 1997 three companies—Johnson & Johnson, Boston Scientific, and Arterial Vascular Engineering—had been accustomed to dividing the spoils in this $1.3 billion per year market amongst themselves.

IP-savvy M&As can offer patent-protected entry into lucrative new markets.

But all that changed in October 1997 when Guidant launched a daring assault on the patent-protected shores of stent-land. The first shots in what analysts came to call "stent mania" were fired on October 2, 1997, when Guidant received FDA approval for its new Multi-Link stent. Understandably horrified at the thought of having to divide $1.3 billion by 4 instead of 3, Johnson & Johnson rallied its rapid-deployment force of legal commandos and in less than 24 hours slapped Guidant with a patent infringement suit. Its tenuous beachhead in the stent market threatened, Guidant responded three days later with a surprise flanking maneuver: rather than filing a patent countersuit of its own, Guidant instead bought EndoVascular Technologies.

But why? EndoVascular didn't even make stents. Reporter Herb Greenberg, then writing for the *San Francisco Chronicle,* revealed the answer in his October 8, 1997, column: "What nobody talks about is patents. [Guidant] will also be getting its hands on a potentially lucrative patent that could give [it] control over the super-heated U.S. coronary stent market."[8]

The deal, it turns out, included an unused EndoVascular stent patent that may prove to be a legal bombshell by virtue of having been issued *two years earlier* than Johnson & Johnson's patent. Does Guidant now hold a winning weapon in the stent wars? It remains to be seen which company will eventually prevail in court. But doubtless Guidant already feels that the $170 million it paid for EndoVascular and its key stent patent was money well spent, for in its first six months in the stent business, the company sold $350 million worth of the devices.

Triple the Patents Equals Six Times the Market Value

Yesterday's daring market invader, of course, can easily become today's harried market defender. Such was Guidant's fate eight months later when its control of the market for rapid-exchange catheters, which enable the more efficient exchange of balloons during procedures such as angioplasty, was challenged by the toughest M&A player of all: Boston Scientific (BSC). In June 1998, BSC acquired Pfizer's Schneider unit for $2.1 billion. According to the *Wall Street Journal,* "Boston Scientific's interest in Schneider lies in the Pfizer unit's strong intellectual property portfolio, which includes patents for rapid-exchange catheters."[9]

In its early years, BSC never initiated acquisitions. But owing to the rapid pace of change in medical markets, explains company CFO Larry Best, BSC found it "needed to accelerate [its market entry] programs for fear that we might get left behind."[10] So in late 1994, BSC began a 16-month, nine-company buying spree that opened up several new markets for the company, increased its storehouse of patents from 190 to 600, and boosted its market capitalization from $1.5 billion at the end of 1994 to a whopping $8.5 billion one year later—a fine example of the sort of "multiplication by addition" that patent-driven M&As make possible.

Poor Guidant. Barely did it have time to catch its breath after BSC's takeover of Schneider than another of its rivals, Arterial Vascular Engineering (AVE), joined the fray by nabbing C.R. Bard and its catheter patents for $550 million. AVE was thereafter purchased by Medtronic for $3.7 billion, thus turning a market that had once been dominated solely by Guidant into a three-way brawl among Guidant, BSC, and Medtronic.

IP Tools for M&A "Grow" Strategies

Is your company looking to get the jump on a new market-leading technology that could reshape your industry? Do you want to find the next Amati or the next WebTV before competitors even know what hit them? You may discover just the opportunity you're looking for hidden inside today's electronic patent databases.

Imagine, for example, that Intel is interested in the new market for handheld "information appliances," which have been touted of late as the "next big thing" in computing. To be sure, its main interest lies in developing the microprocessors for such devices, but Intel often seeds the growth of emerging market opportunities by investing in related technologies. Many handheld appliances and other Net-enabled electronic devices employ embedded real-time operating systems that are designed for the most part by small, under $100 million companies—firms that are potentially vulnerable to acquisition. A Patent Hit Count by Assignee for embedded real-time operating system technologies would list firms doing the most extensive work in this field. Further analysis of the patents, as well as the business and financial profiles of the firms to which they have been assigned, might then shine the light on a creditable acquisition target.

Another example—this time of an actual IP-driven M&A Grow strategy in action—is offered by the chip maker Via Technologies, which had staked its future on a new line of speedy, low-cost Intel-compatible chip sets. In June 1999, however, industry giant Intel attempted to derail Via's plans by revoking its patent license agreement with the upstart chip maker and slapping it with an infringement suit. But Via devised a plan to get around the Intel blockade: it bought the Cyrix chip-making division of National Semiconductor, which does have an Intel license arrangement. So now, with National Semiconductor's manufacturing support, Via is able to move aggressively into this fast-growing and lucrative new market.

PUTTING THE "FIX" ON CHIP MERGERS

Nothing is so conducive to merger mania, of course, as the uncertainty caused by a major industry realignment. Precisely such a realignment has rocked the semiconductor industry of late as a result of a growing tension between the demand for ever-more powerful and complex chips and the intensifying need to reduce their cost and time to market. This contradiction has sparked vendor demand for reusable chip "building blocks" (i.e., the designs themselves) that can be integrated into a variety of products as needed. As a result, chip design firms have suddenly become the key link in the industry value chain—and their intellectual property, their patented designs, are now seen as the key to competitive advantage. The resulting flurry of mergers and acquisitions aimed at acquiring control of key chip design patents—either to plug competitive gaps in companies' IP portfolios or to outflank competitors—offers some interesting case studies of IP-driven M&A Fix strategies at work.

Outflanking the Giant

In early 1998, S3 was a small chip design firm with a big problem. The company knew that its high-performance graphic chip business would eventually become the object of industry giant Intel's fear or envy, and hence it was only a matter of time before it would be hit with the threat of an infringement suit. So S3 hatched a plan to fix the problem.

Acting anonymously, S3 outbid Intel at auction to acquire the patents of bankrupt chip maker Exponential Technologies for $10 million, thereby getting its hands on a patent that predated Intel's Merced chip patents and could potentially hold Intel's next-generation processor business hostage. S3's bold IP gambit paid off when it revealed itself as the buyer and forced Intel to reluctantly cross-license its patents to S3 in exchange for S3's promise not to challenge Intel's Merced patents.

A Marriage Made in Patent Court

Over in the tool sector of the design business, meanwhile, Quickturn Design Systems also had a problem that needed fixing. Having sued rival Mentor Graphics for patent infringement and gotten an injunction that blocked U.S. sales of Mentor's key product, Quickturn now faced a hostile Mentor bid to acquire it and thereby scuttle the injunction. Quickturn resisted, of course, and the two companies battled back and forth through the summer and fall of 1998. Quickturn knew it could not fend off Mentor's advances forever, however, so it dropped its intellectual property hankie (as it were) in front of white knight Cadence Design Systems, which responded with a $253 million buyout offer that the much-relieved Quickturn happily accepted. Its flanks no longer exposed to hostile M&A action from Mentor, Quickturn continued to press its infringement case until Mentor agreed in June 1999 to withdraw its SimExpress product from the market.

IP Tools for M&A "Fix" Strategies

One of the most common aims of M&A Fix strategies is to strengthen competitive weaknesses in a firm's patent position. A Patent Landscape Map can help locate an acquisition target that can reinforce your technology strength.

For example, Figure 6-1, shows the competitive position of a multibillion dollar chemical firm's patent holdings versus that of its chief rival. Both companies must remain unnamed. The small white dots on the map show that the firm is weak in elastomer technology, with only two patents in that technology area. The window panel at the left side of the map, however, indicates that its rival has 138 elastomer patents (out of a combined total for both companies of 140 patents in this technology).

Assuming that elastomers do, in fact, represent a strategic business opportunity for this chemical firm, then acquisitions analysis should begin with a survey of the patent positions of the dozens of other chemical companies that together hold over 8,000 patents in the elastomer field. Such an analysis will reveal that the elastomer patent landscape is broadly dispersed among

FIGURE 6-1 LANDSCAPE MAP COMPARING TWO FORTUNE 100 COMPANIES' PATENT PORTFOLIOS

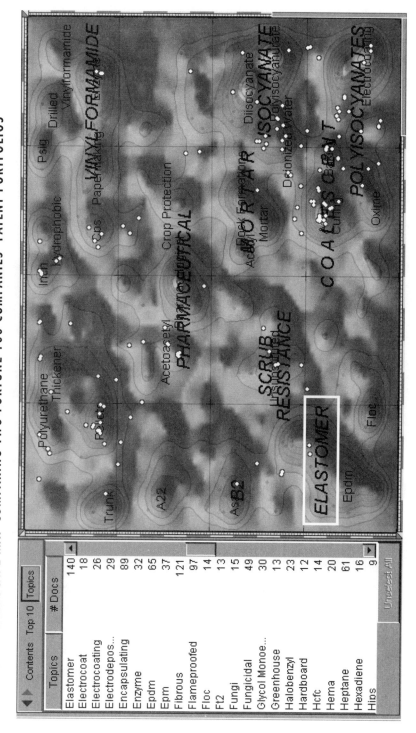

Source: Chart courtesy of Aurigin Systems, Inc., using ThemeScape™ software module.

a wide array of small and midsized firms—fertile ground, in other words, for acquisition candidates. A wise approach in this case might be to look for firms with patent holdings that are large enough to be of use—Kao Corporation and the Glidden Company each have 36 elastomer patents, for example—yet still small enough that your buyout offer would be unlikely to attract competing bids from your competitors. With an aggressive acquisition effort such as this, our elastomer-challenged chemical firm could eventually outflank its rival in this technology field.

Another common goal of M&A Fix strategies is to buy companies with underutilized patent portfolios that can be tapped for incremental revenues through licensing. That's precisely what STMicroelectronics did when it bought Mostek for $71 million and managed to squeeze out $450 million in licensing royalties within seven years.[11]

But where are the Mosteks of the world today, and how does one find them? One place to look would be at distressed companies such as Zenith, whose staggering losses have already sparked discussion among analysts over what the venerable old TV maker should do. "Zenith must scrap its manufacturing operations," argued Robert Gutenstein of Kalb Voorhis & Company, "and recast itself as a designer and marketer of products using its digital television patents and its well-recognized brand name."[12]

Not a bad idea at all, actually. But if Zenith doesn't have the good sense to recast its business focus around the extensive intellectual property portfolio it has developed over the years, perhaps another company does. If not, then Zenith's name will probably pop up sooner or later in bankruptcy filings, which is another place to look for potential Mosteks. Few firms facing bankruptcy would even think of taking the TM Patents approach (see Chapter 5) and exploiting the value of their untapped patent holdings. Thus, the task here is to find out which of these firms have IP portfolios and then evaluate the patents in question for their potential license value.

An additional place to look for underleveraged and acquirable patent assets might be the IP portfolios of very large diversified companies that have either shifted their business focus in recent years or seem to be having trouble integrating their disparate lines of business. In the 1980s, you may recall, a number of telephone companies diversified into real estate, financial services, and other ventures unrelated to their core businesses—all of which failed and were sold off at fire-sale prices. There may be similar patent-based opportunities among today's overextended diversifiers.

Another intriguing M&A opportunity may exist among the many e-commerce firms that are already beginning to reel from industry shakeout and consolidation pressures. In the next year or so, there are going to be a lot of "Dot.com DOAs" just waiting to be picked up. A Patent Count by Assignee can reveal the patent holdings of firms that appear to be failing.

Figure 6-2a, for example, shows the patent landscape in various kinds of e-commerce transaction processing software. Figure 6-2b shows the individual patent counts for firms such as IBM, MasterCard, Citibank, and others. We guarantee you that many of the smaller firms will not survive, at least in their present form. They simply don't have the banking, retailing, or other channel partnership deals necessary for success. Their patents, however, might prove to be valuable either competitively or as vehicles for generating licensing revenue.

Don't wait too long, however, or the best deals may soon be taken. Renowned venture capitalist Roger McNamee has just formed the first-ever technology-focused leveraged buyout firm. Silver Lake Partners raised a billion-dollar fund to buy up high-tech firms that have either fallen out of favor with investors or have major technology assets they have failed to exploit. Sources close to the firm say it is targeting not only underperforming divisions of large firms, but divisions with patents that could be "worth a fortune if enforced."[13]

FIGURE 6-2a E-COMMERCE PATENTS IN "TRANSACTION MOUNTAIN"

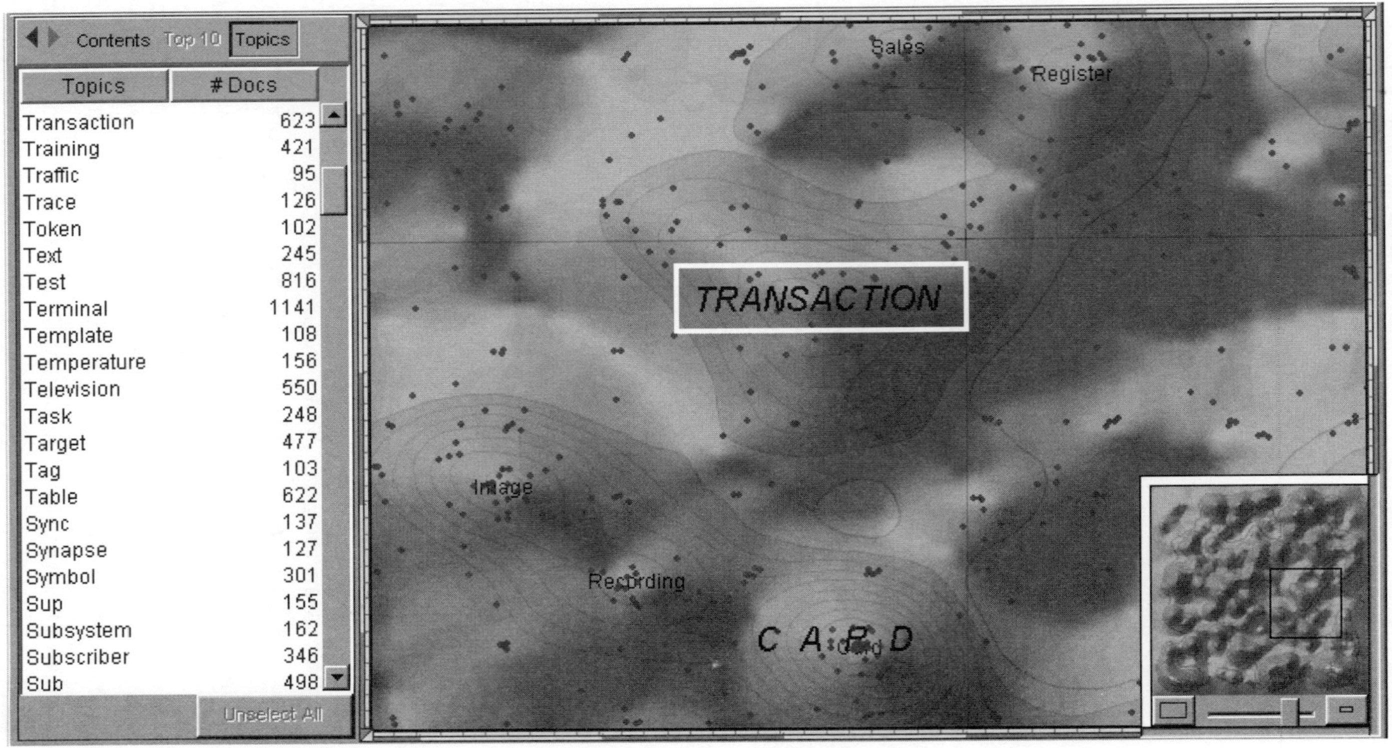

Topics	# Docs
Transaction	623
Training	421
Traffic	95
Trace	126
Token	102
Text	245
Test	816
Terminal	1141
Template	108
Temperature	156
Television	550
Task	248
Target	477
Tag	103
Table	622
Sync	137
Synapse	127
Symbol	301
Sup	155
Subsystem	162
Subscriber	346
Sub	498

Source: Chart courtesy of Aurigin Systems, Inc., using ThemeScape™ software module.

FIGURE 6-2b   PATENT COUNT BY ASSIGNEE FOR TRANSACTION MOUNTAIN

Assignee	Document Count
Citibank, N.A.	10
Omron Tateisi Electronics Co.	9
International Business Machines Corporation	7
Fujitsu Limited	6
Hitachi, Ltd.	6
MasterCard International, Inc.	6
Visa International Service Association	4
Merrill Lynch, Pierce, Fenner & Smith Incorporated	3
NCR Corporation	3
Amazon.Com, Inc.	2
AT&T Bell Laboratories	2
AT&T Corp.	2
Bell Communications Research, Inc.	2
College Savings Bank	2
Commonweal Incorporated	2
Data Card Corporation	2
Foreign Exchange Transaction Services, Inc.	2
Lucent Technologies Inc.	2
Reuters Limited	2
Sharp Kabushiki Kaisha	2
Telepay	2
Wright Technologies, L.P.	2
Ad Response MicroMarketing Corporation	1
American Savings Bank, F.A.	1
Arbor International, Inc.	1
Arris, Inc.	1
AT&T IPM Corp.	1

Source: Courtesy of Aurigin Systems, Inc.

"SELL" STRATEGIES THAT DIVIDE AND CONQUER

Does your company possess technologies that are noncore to the business? Do you have an underperforming business unit that has proved impervious to all attempts at fixing? Then consider the Sell strategy employed by aerospace firm Lockheed Martin.

Over the years, Lockheed had assembled a cache of 3D flight simulator patents, but by 1997 these were simply gathering dust in the corporate legal office. Working with investment bank Hambrecht & Quist, however, Lockheed created a new venture called Real3D built around the patents and then spun it off to compete in the fast-growing PC graphics and video game business. It soon attracted investments from Intel and Silicon Graphics, and is currently valued at several hundred million dollars. Thus a group of fallow patents valued on Lockheed's books at exactly zero was turned into a 40 percent stake in Real3D that is today worth upward of $100 million; in addition, the move provided the aerospace giant with a strategic presence in the graphics chip industry.

Patent Tools That Help You Sell to Win

If your goal is to sell off a unit of your company that is failing or no longer strategic to your business, the IP analysis challenge is to find companies with similar or related technologies that could blend your technology assets synergistically with their own. A Patent Citation Tree (similar to Figure 3-7) will turn up companies whose patents have cited your patents—or vice versa—and for which your patents might fill some competitive gaps in their portfolios.

Just such a Patent Citation Tree was employed recently by a major chemical firm in the divestiture of one of its business units. According to a spokesman for the company (which wishes to remain anonymous), automated IP analysis tools helped them find and close the deal in a third less time and at a 20 percent higher price, which was worth "millions of dollars to us."

HOW TO CONDUCT IP-SAVVY DUE DILIGENCE

Patent analysis can help companies not only uncover ripe M&A activities, but also make sure these are truly the best opportunities. This is no small matter, for most corporate due diligence efforts in intellectual property matters are simply abysmal. Indeed, it is the rare company—and the even rarer investment bank or M&A firm—that has any clue whatsoever about how to value, analyze, and structure the IP asset transfers involved in a merger, acquisition, or divestiture.

"I'd say—and I'm speaking very generally now—that patent analysis is usually just a pro forma component of the due diligence process in most M&As," admits a senior executive at one of Wall Street's leading investment banks, who insisted on remaining anonymous. "Most M&A firms, including ours, simply don't look closely at the patent portfolios involved, either for valuation issues or for exploitation possibilities."

Most investment banks have teams of accountants, tax advisors, management consultants, and regulatory affairs experts to structure their deals to greatest advantage. But one would be hard pressed to find a major investment bank that employs even one individual with experience in evaluating patent portfolios. Doubtless this will change as corporate America and Wall Street become more attuned to the financial and strategic value of intellectual property, but as matters stand now, "due diligence" regarding patent assets is usually more myth than reality.

"You have to spend time and money in order to satisfy that you are not buying a problem," says Lawrence Graev, a partner at O'Sullivan, Graev & Karabell, "[but] most firms are shirking on conducting a complete intellectual property audit."[14]

Adds Bruce Berman of the IP consulting firm Brody Berman Associates, "Patents being used for income is a relatively new development, and I guarantee buyout firms are not thinking about that."[15]

Digging Beneath the Patent Surface

Cynthia O'Donohue is Principal Information Specialist for the global pharmaceutical company Allergan, responsible for evaluating patent and other intellectual property issues and advising on mergers and acquisitions strategy. Over the course of her career, O'Donohue has also managed R&D, run manufacturing operations, and conducted acquisitions analysis for some of the biggest companies in America, including Philip Morris. In short, she knows what she's talking about when it comes to patent issues.

"Upper management may say that patent analysis is critical in acquisitions, but they don't do it nearly as well as they should," she said. "For example, if you're looking to acquire or merge with a company, you have to ask, 'How does their technology fit in with ours? Is it compatible? Does it fill any missing gaps in our own technology?' This is where patent analysis must start. You go in and look at their patents, and very quickly you can see if, for example, their patents covering psoriasis treatments complement your patents covering acne treatments.

"But that's not all you need to do," O'Donohue continues. "Sure, you may see that they have all these wonderful patents, but you have to ask, 'When do they expire?' It may seem obvious, but most companies actually don't do that. And you have to ask not only when they expire, but, especially if you're looking to acquire a smaller company, you have to ask if they've maintained their patents. Because if the maintenance fees are not paid, then those patents have elapsed. And I'm not just talking in the U.S., either, but worldwide. Have they maintained those patents in every country where the patent has been issued?

"And there's still more to be done. Can you invalidate the patents, find loopholes or improper claims or prior art errors in them? Because if you can invalidate them, so can someone else. And then what about the engineers? The key executives? Are they going to remain once the company is acquired? Because it's not just the patents, but the human expertise behind them that you want."

Unfortunately, says O'Donohue, "companies don't always look closely at these patent issues, even in the pharmaceutical industry. And so all too often, when these patent portfolios are being acquired, they're not even valid patents."

Doesn't she find that a bit shocking, especially in an industry such as pharmaceuticals where companies live or die on the strength of their patent positions?

O'Donohue sighs. "If you knew what I know about how some companies acquire other companies—how they conduct their due diligence—you'd be even more shocked."

This situation is unfortunate, she believes, because companies can benefit greatly by a thorough due diligence effort where patents are concerned. She offers an example.

"When I was at Philip Morris, there was a little company that we were thinking of acquiring," she recalls. "They had a small but important patent position in the technology we wanted, or so we thought. After reviewing the patents, however, we discovered that the claims on them were written too narrowly. This is not that unusual with small companies; they often don't get the patent protection they should from their lawyers. Anyway, because the claims were so narrowly drawn on these patents, we felt that competitors could patent around them. In other words, this company did not have the preemptive position in the technology that we thought they had, so it wasn't worth spending all the money to buy them."

The end result? "In this case we killed the deal," she says. "We saved a lot of money and avoided getting in a situation where we'd have to defend patents that couldn't be defended."

Another critic of most corporate due diligence efforts regarding patents is Sam Khoury, the former intellectual asset manager at Dow Chemical (see Chapter 3) who is now president of the IP management firm Consor. He tells of one particularly eye-opening experience he had when trying to analyze some polypropylene patents that Dow wished to acquire from a European firm. Though this was a licensing transaction, the issues would be the same in a merger, acquisition, or joint venture.

"In 1996, this company offered to license a package of polypropylene patents to us for $18 million," Khoury recalls. "But when we asked for a list of the particular patents included in the package, they told us no. 'Why do you want to know?' they asked. 'No one else ever asked.'"

No other company had asked to see a list of the patents involved?

"No, most companies wouldn't ask," Khoury laughs. "That's how bad most companies are at thinking about intellectual property. Anyway, I found out this company had already licensed these patents to many other firms—and even more important, that they had been licensing this package for seven years already. Had some of those patents expired already? There was no way to know—not without seeing them."

After much arguing back and forth, the licensing firm finally agreed to let Dow see a list of the individual patents. But the price was nonnegotiable. No matter what the evaluation revealed, Dow would have to pay $18 million if it wanted that package of patents. "Once we got the list of patents," Khoury relates, "we discovered that the most critical ones only had three years until they expired. And some of the less important ones were even going to expire sooner—in six months!" Nonetheless, Dow felt it needed the patents. But given the "depreciation" on some of them, how could the company get more value for its $18 million?

"I went to our competitive intelligence people," Khoury recalls, "and asked them to find out more about the firm's recent research in polypropylene catalysts. We learned that they had ten new patents that were not included in the package. These were unproven technologies, still in the research lab, but they looked pretty good. So we told them we'd pay the $18 million, but they had to include these ten new patents in the package. And that's what they did."

Beware of "Deferred Maintenance" Dangers

If you were looking to buy a home, wouldn't you want to know how well the property had been maintained by its current owner? Even the most unsophisticated buyer would be wary upon discovering dry rot or termite problems that had been ignored and left untreated for years. And yet supposedly cutting-edge technology firms are bought every week in deals in which the buyer never bothers to check how sharp that "cutting-edge" technology really is.

Has the target company's rate of patenting declined in recent years? Are its patents being cited less often by other firms (an indication that its technology is not as innovative as it once was)? Are the citations in its own patents getting old, suggesting a slowing in the company's pace of technological innovation? Are its patents encumbered by restrictive license agreements or infringement suits? Has it simply neglected to pay the required maintenance fees on its patents, thereby allowing them to expire?

Hard as it may be to believe, most acquiring companies never even ask such questions. And they certainly don't use any of the patent analysis tools that could help answer those questions, such as an Innovation Strength report showing how often a firm's patents are cited by others, or an Innovation Cycle Speed report indicating its pace of innovation compared to that of other companies in its industry.

For unlike situations in which physical assets such as a home are being purchased, it is rarely worth acquiring a company with deferred maintenance problems in its patented technology holdings. If the selling company failed to file patents on its next-generation core product technologies, or if the firm delayed even doing the R&D on that next generation of products because it wanted to save money in preparation for a sale, then there's little you can do. And if the firm is likely to be the subject of a patent infringement suit—or, indeed, has already been hit with such a suit—you could be buying more trouble than you ever bargained for. In 1992, for instance, the buyout firm Jordan Company acquired LePage's, a maker of Post-it–like products and adhesive tape. Unfortunately for the Jordan Co., however, a patent suit filed by 3M stopped LePage's from developing and selling its products, and even seven years later, the Jordan Co. is still mired in litigation over it.[16]

Don't Forget the Human Element

Finally, don't forget that it's not just the intellectual property you want, but the engineers and inventors who created it as well. In his 1996 book *Competitive Intelligence,* author Larry Kahaner tells of a company so interested in another firm's patented technology that it offered to buy the company. The offer was accepted, but all did not end well:

> Had the [acquiring] company done more competitive intelligence homework, they would have discovered that all the patents for this technology were in the name of one scientist, and that particular scientist had moved to another firm months before the acquisition offer. So while the buyer got use of the current technology . . . it didn't [get] the promise of future technology advances as it had expected.[17]

Checklist for IP Due Diligence

If you want to make sure that your next high-tech acquisition doesn't buy you a pig in a patent poke, keep the following checklist of questions in mind. And remember, what follows is only a checklist and therefore is no substitute for rigorous and informed due diligence of IP assets:

- Expirations?

- Claims and prior art errors?

- Maintenance fees paid?

- Valid in what countries?

- Deferred maintenance?

- Pending infringement actions?

- Engineers on board?

- Next-generation technologies patented?

- Encumbering licenses?

- Royalty potential?

- Innovation speed and strength?

CONFIGURING INTELLECTUAL PROPERTY ASSET SALES

Once you've found your buyer or seller and conducted the proper due diligence on the IP assets involved in the deal, it's time to structure the deal to take advantage of the many legal, tax, and other advantages that are uniquely available to IP asset sales.

Many firms don't realize, for example, that intellectual property rights can be configured in ways that the sale of, say, machine tools cannot—by geography, for example, or by market or product line. A firm selling off its inkjet technology patents as part of the divestiture of its copier division, for example, could limit those rights by line of business or product so as to ensure that the rights sold don't later come back to bite the nose of its printer division. Alternatively, the patent rights could be sold for use only in European markets, or with the restriction that these rights never be sublicensed to any of the seller's competitors.

Intellectual property asset sales can also be structured in ways that separate the legal from the economic rights to a patent portfolio. This division could enable an acquiring company to get the best of both worlds, as it were: the strict legal protection for patents that exists in the United States, as well as the lower tax levies found in some other countries. Dan Giannini, a mergers and acquisitions specialist for PriceWaterhouseCoopers, offers an example.

"One prominent case where this was done involved an acquisition by a semiconductor manufacturer here in the U.S.," Giannini recalls. "They placed the economic rights to the intellectual property with a technology holding company in Hong Kong, because of its very low tax rate—generally around 17 percent or so. By moving the income they were generating from their intellectual property to Hong Kong, they were able to lower their effective tax rate on it by about 15 percent." This is not an insignificant savings, especially for companies with active patent licensing programs. A firm with $70 million a year in license royalties, for example, could save over $10 million in taxes through such a move.

Unlike real property, the sale of IP assets can be restricted by geography or line of business.

And finally, any company selling intellectual property must be careful to indemnify itself against any future use of the technology by the buyer that infringes a third party's patents. We cannot stress enough the potential for liability from *contributory* infringement—especially in the Internet e-commerce sector, where everyone is essentially competing with everyone else and where *per use*-based damage awards for infringement could destroy your company overnight (see Chapter 7).

Preparation and execution are the hallmarks of successful M&A deals, and it is no longer acceptable to ignore intellectual property analysis—especially where patent assets make up the bulk of a firm's asset wealth. Patent analysis can be of enormous help in locating the right M&A or joint venture opportunity, just as it can assist you in conducting the all-important due diligence process properly. And given the mania for mergers these days, a significant share of which fail to achieve the results desired, intellectual property's value as both asset and business tool may provide your company with just the edge it needs to achieve your business development objectives.

7

SURVIVING THE
INTERNET PATENT WARS

Two men. Each a respected innovator. Yet each with a radically different vision of intellectual property's role in the future of Internet commerce.

Jay Walker

"All of the world's business systems are being reinvented in light of the Internet," declares Jay Walker, chairman of Walker Digital, an "intellectual property laboratory" modeled after Thomas Edison's nineteenth-century New Jersey "invention laboratory." But whereas Edison's lab concentrated on inventing the practical apparatus of an industrial economy, Walker's lab is dedicated to creating the more conceptual tools of a knowledge economy.

"Walker Digital is about reengineering the DNA of

the future of business," he explains. "What we hope is that a group of thoughtful people can together reinvent whole sectors of the global economy. And not only can we reinvent them, we can *own* those inventions."[1]

New business models for a new economy. New business models that can be *owned*. Does this mean that a company's future business could end up being controlled by someone else?

"The answer is yes," warns Walker.[2]

Of course, the reverse is also true. A patent for a new business idea could become a ticket to extraordinary wealth and success, especially in the e-commerce sector of the Internet, where success depends more on innovative new methods of doing business than on capital or other traditional inputs. Indeed, an e-commerce business model patent could become a sort of a deed to a piece of the underlying architecture of the twenty-first-century economy itself.

On the Net, it's no longer who is first to market, but who is first to patent.

This was apparently the vision motivating the venture capitalists who invested $100 million in Walker's first spin-off company, Priceline.com. It also explains why they allowed him to spend an unprecedented $2.5 million—250 times the usual cost—to pursue the key patent for Priceline's buyer-driven model of auctioning airline tickets. And patent No. 5,794,207 certainly seems solid, at least compared with the many trash patents these days that cite little or no prior art in their fields. Priceline's patent contains 10 patent and 11 nonpatent prior art citations.

It does face challenges, however: one from an inventor who claims that he applied for a similar patent before Walker did, and another from a now-defunct firm that insists it ran buyer-driven auctions via fax a decade ago. But so far, investors seem confident that these challenges will be defeated. During the March 1999 public offering of Priceline stock, they bid the price up 435 percent, valuing the firm at nearly $10 billion—more than the value of United, Continental, and Northwest Airlines combined. Two months later, Priceline was worth nearly $20 billion.

Even by Internet standards, this is an extraordinary valuation for a firm that lost $114 million on $35 million in sales in 1998. According to the *Wall Street Journal,* it also "spotlights the extent to which Priceline.com's fortunes are tied to a new model of electronic commerce."[3] But it's not just a "new model" of e-commerce—it's a *patented* new model. And as BancBoston Robertson Stephens analyst Lauren Cooks Levitan points out, "[Priceline's] patents have probably served as a deterrent, because I don't know of anyone that's taken [them] on."[4]

All of which may suggest a shift in the traditional route to Net success. The advantage used to belong to whoever got to market first. Tomorrow it may belong to whoever stakes a defensible patent claim first. Or as a *Forbes* profile of Jay Walker put it, "Get a patent, start a business."[5]

Bruce Perens

Meanwhile, in another corner of the Web, software programmer Bruce Perens isn't quite sure whether he's sitting on top of the world or stuck between a rock and a hard place.

On the one hand, Perens and his colleagues in the Open Source Initiative—a loose confederation of volunteer developers whose free, collaboratively developed software (or "freeware") forms the infrastructure of the Internet—are finally getting the recognition they deserve, thanks to the extraordinary success of Linux. Linux is a free computer operating system, originally created by Linus Torvalds at the University of Helsinki in 1991, that many believe poses the first serious challenge to Microsoft hegemony in nearly a decade. Some of the biggest hardware and software companies in the world, in fact, have jumped on the Linux bandwagon in the past year, either adapting versions of their own software to work with Linux or offering Linux as an alternative to Microsoft's Windows NT on certain high-end computers and network servers. To Perens and other developers, this mainstream corporate embrace of Linux represents the first *commercial* validation of the Open Source credo that sometimes the best way to produce superior software is to freely give away the software's source code—its intellectual property core—and then invite the best programming minds in the world to tinker with and improve it.

"Open Source refutes the conventional notion that people won't invent unless they have the incentive of patents," says Perens. "It's just not always true, at least not on the Net."

And he's right—to a point. After all, the Internet itself was largely created by university-based software developers who cared not a whit either for patents or profits. The problem for Perens and other Open Source developers, however, is that their very success in constructing a commercially viable Internet has now spawned an on-line patenting gold rush of epic proportions. Small start-ups and giant corporations alike are racing to stake claims to proprietary positions along the booming e-commerce frontier. In 1998 alone, the Patent and Trademark Office issued 2,193 Internet patents, an increase of more than 300 percent over the number granted in 1997. And those numbers don't include the 22,930 separately classified software patents related to data processing, networking, and communications that were issued that same year, a 40 percent jump from the year before.

"Many in the industry say they have never seen anything like the onslaught of today's patent gold rush," noted one on-line news report.[6] But as the saying goes, they ain't seen nothing yet. For although a few skirmishes over patent rights have already broken out on the Net, the patent wars won't really start to get bloody until late 1999 or the year 2000, when the huge backlog of Internet patent applications still awaiting PTO approval are finally granted.

In the view of Perens and many of his colleagues, these numbers add up to big trouble. In fact, they fear that today's Internet patenting stampede could end up crushing them under the litigious hooves of a herd of lawsuit-wielding patent lawyers and cordoning off their once wide-open cyberspace frontier with thousands of intellectual property fences.

"There's a tremendous amount of concern within the community that these patents will be used to close out avenues for free software development," explains Perens, who just launched his own start-up company. "Many technologies that we'd like to use on Linux workstations—Web browser plug-ins, for example—are patented. So if I want to distribute a free Web browser, I have to handicap it by not including a plug-in, or else I risk being sued.

"Patents," he warns, "may become the next great battle for the Linux community."

Two men. Two opposing views of intellectual property. But only one Internet, whose competitive dynamics are now being shaped by the intensifying conflict between these two approaches. If it does come to open warfare—and the May 1999 call by the World Wide Web's inventor Tim Berners-Lee for developers to fight the patent system suggests that it very well might—will Open Source developers be able to survive it? Or will they be forced to the sidelines of software creation by a barrage of patent suits, eventually becoming little more than quaint relics of bygone cottage-

Use patents to secure and defend a profitable position in the e-commerce economy.

industry days on the Net? The answer is not at all clear. For while it is true that the power and influence of intellectual property are growing inexorably worldwide, the Internet economy also contains some unique features that, properly exploited, may enable the Open Source model of software development to survive even in a world where patents rule.

Whatever the future holds for Open Source developers, their looming conflict with patent-holding businesses spotlights crucial strategy issues that anyone doing business on the Internet must consider. These issues not only get to the heart of what is unique about the dynamics of business competition on the Net, but also illuminate the special challenges that companies will face in developing patent strategies that truly enhance their success in the complex and still-evolving landscape of Internet commerce.

In this chapter, we discuss the challenges companies face in trying to leverage the power of patents to help secure, enhance, and defend a proprietary stake in the burgeoning e-commerce economy. We examine the unique economic and competitive power of patents in this new Internet environment and assess the special challenge that the Open Source movement poses for patent-holding enterprises. Finally, we suggest ways that businesses may be able to adapt their IP strategies to that challenge and turn it to competitive advantage, thereby solidifying their market position and reducing their risk of becoming just another "Dot.com DOA" on the landscape of the New Economy.

THE UNIQUE POWER OF INTERNET PATENTS

First, however, it's necessary to grasp the extraordinary scale of the e-commerce market opportunity as well as the unprecedented power and reach—not to mention the dangers—that today's Internet patents hold for those who wish to exploit this opportunity.

An Unprecedented Market Opportunity

One factor unique to today's Internet patenting stampede is the sheer size of the market stakes involved: tens of billions of dollars in on-line sales already, with hundreds of billions of dollars more to come in just the next few years. According to a recent survey of CEOs by PriceWaterhouseCoopers, 40 percent said they expect e-commerce to account for more than 10 percent of their companies' revenues over the next five years, and half of that 40 percent estimate e-commerce will exceed 20 percent of total revenue. All told, Forrester Research projects total e-commerce revenues of $3.2 *trillion* by the year 2003. That's about 5 percent of all global sales, or an amount nearly equal to Japan's entire GDP.[7]

Even those numbers, unprecedented as they are for an industry that is barely five years old, don't capture the scale and scope of the stakes involved for business as electronic commerce reshapes and reconstitutes nearly every industry on earth. Consider, for example, that U.S. businesses today are sitting on approximately $1 trillion worth of inventory—and that at least *half* of that $1 trillion, say experts, can be freed up through Net-enabled improvements in supply chain management. Now extend that sort of trillion-dollar "e-engineering" opportunity across every business sector—from retailing to manufacturing to services—and then into every business function—from customer service and order processing to supplier and partner transactions—and we're talking about the greatest economic transformation, the biggest upsurge in capital liberation and wealth creation, in history.

But as *Business Week* noted, "To take full advantage of this opportunity, [businesses have] to reinvent the way they do business—changing how they distribute goods, collaborate inside the company, and deal with suppliers."[8]

The change has already begun. General Electric has already

cut 15 percent of its supply costs as a result of electronic purchasing over the Net. Other companies have automated their sales, customer support, and other processes to great economic and competitive effect. Perhaps no company is further along in the reinvention of its business than Cisco Systems, however. It now earns 70 percent of total sales from the Net, which also serves as a platform for Cisco's product manufacturing and design.

With distribution costs crashing toward zero, and access to millions of customers now possible through the mere click of a mouse, the term "economies of scale" has taken on a whole new meaning. Indeed, the old joke about "losing a dollar on every sale but making it up in volume" has suddenly become deadly serious marketing strategy as more than a few companies—not the least of them being Microsoft—actually give away their products in a frenzied race for market share. Because once a company has secured a market foothold and some brand allegiance from Net users, it seems that they really can "make it up in volume" with their next product upgrade—no longer free, of course. It's the "Law of Large Numbers" on steroids.

All these luscious new markets and heaving revenues at stake leave CEOs trembling, of course, although whether in fear or anticipation is not always clear. For if the scale of this opportunity is indeed quite unprecedented, so is the power of today's new Internet patents to either help or hinder companies trying to capitalize on that opportunity.

Interlinked Net Architecture Enhances Patent Clout

Consider, for example, that because of the interlinked architecture of the Internet economy, digital computer technology has now burrowed its way into every industry and sector of the economy. This gives today's patents a reach and power they never had before—and not just business-method patents, either. Indeed, even a patent for a simple software application may now affect the fortunes of hundreds of companies in dozens of industries if its owner decides to demand licensing fees.

The power and reach of e-commerce patents are further enhanced by the interlinked Net's tendency to dissolve the traditional dividing lines between industries. "E-commerce has created an environment where many companies, at a very modest cost, could compete with us in very short order," concedes Phil Fasano, executive VP at Deutsche Financial Services in St. Louis.[9] For example, is Amazon.com a book seller, record and video distributor, auction house, pet store, or direct marketing firm—or all of the above? All anyone knows for sure is that everyone is suddenly competing with everyone else on-line. Barnes and Noble learned what it was like to be "Amazoned"—losing customers to Internet upstarts— and many other companies have as well.

What's your barrier to competitors—your defense against being "Amazoned?"

What's your barrier to entry, your defense against being Amazoned? In the no-holds-barred competitive slug-fest that is the Internet today, patents can become your only shield—your only defense and proprietary advantage against bigger or better-financed competitors.

Ironically, Amazon.com itself may soon learn that lesson, for its blockbuster brand—its sole competitive advantage—may now be in danger of being diluted by the company's recent acquisitions binge and new market expansions. Many of its most loyal users no longer feel an emotional tie to what was once an upstart bookstore thumbing its nose at the giant chains, if only because Amazon.com is no longer just a bookstore. And if Amazon.com loses that brand equity, what does it have left?

Just three patents—none of them strategic, and all involving credit card processing technologies that more powerful players have patented more effectively. One has to wonder what Amazon's lawyers were thinking when they recommended filing for these patents. What was the *business* purpose here? Amazon's commercial fortunes would have been far better served had it patented technologies truly strategic to its business, such as the one-click ordering system that the company pioneered and that is used widely by on-line retailers today. That was a real business-method choke point (see Chapter 4) that Amazon could have controlled to no small advantage. But as it is, without that proprietary advantage and with its brand strength eroding, companies like Virgin Records and PetSmart are unafraid to compete directly against the giant on-line retailer. Don't be surprised if Amazon's stock market fortunes head south when investors realize this fact.

Net Patents Have Great Value

This expanded competitve clout also enhances Net patents' economic value—and precisely at a time when the asset value of all forms of intellectual property is skyrocketing in every sector of the economy. To appreciate just how dramatically the value of intellectual property has grown in recent years, consider that in the life span of a single patent—a mere 18 years—the asset base of U.S. manufacturing firms has shifted from one in which physical assets such as plant, equipment, and property constituted 62 percent of their market value in 1982 to one in which such assets represented barely 38 percent of their market value in 1992 and probably less than 30 percent today, according to economists at the Brookings Institution.[10] The great bulk of these firms' value— and these are *manufacturing* companies, mind you—is now made up of intellectual assets.

And when you translate intellectual property's already-greater intrinsic value to a virtual economy such as the Internet, where by definition physical assets are often negligible, a company's proprietary technologies, skills, and business methods may now constitute its entire worth—especially if these are protected by patents. Patents, in fact, are often the only leveragable asset and "collateral" with which a small start-up firm can secure the funding it needs. And once funded, a company will often find that patents may be the only things standing between success and failure. After all, what's to prevent a big company from copying a small start-up's idea, steamrolling over its market space, and eating its entrepreneurial little lunch? Nothing—except, that is, for patents. They are the great equalizers in today's new economy frontier and, as tiny Stac Electronics demonstrated with its $120 million patent victory over Microsoft in 1996, sometimes the only power on earth capable of reducing the financial and marketing might of a corporate behemoth to naught.

Infringement Dangers Abound

If the new power of patents opens up greater opportunities for firms, it also poses new dangers—especially for firms that stumble into a patent infringement situation. Indeed, the interconnected architecture of the Net makes it a virtual patent infringement minefield for IP-unwary firms.

"These Internet patents keep me awake at night," worries Chris Schenken, intellectual property counsel at the $25 billion shipping giant United Parcel Service. "We're concerned about how to avoid stepping on new patents for things that used to exist that are now being done on the Internet." [11] And well he should be, for there are a number of patents either already issued or still pending on methods for accepting credit card information over the Internet, processing orders and transactions of all types, and alerting customers to the

Few companies are even aware of the danger of contributory infringement on the Net.

status of their orders. Without close legal inspection of the claims of these credit card patents, "it's unclear if UPS would have to pay a royalty every time a customer uses a credit card on its Web site," notes *Industry Week*.[12]

True enough, but it is precisely this sort of uncertainty—and potential liability—that businesses abhor.

If major firms such as UPS are already jittery over the danger of direct infringement, just wait until they hear about the *contributory* and *inducement to infringe* provisions of patent law. These provisions hold that a company is not only liable for damages if its own products or services infringe another firm's patents, but it may also be liable if any of the third-party or vendor-supplied technology that it employs in its business infringes on someone else's patents. If your company uses vendor-supplied credit card software to process sales on your e-commerce site, for example, and that vendor is later sued for patent infringement, then you could potentially be sued for contributory infringement as well.

No more than a handful of companies in America are even aware that this contributory infringement peril exists. But they had better wise up, and soon, for the first shot in what could become a Bosnia-like brawl of internecine contributory infringement suits has already been fired. On March 23, 1999, the on-line auction giant eBay was sued by privately held Network Engineering Software (NES) for, in the words of NES attorney Robert Irvine, "using third-party software packages that infringe on NES' patent."[13]

And it gets worse. Even if your company neither directly nor even indirectly employs infringing technology in its business, you could potentially still be sued for inducement to infringe if you help to sell or promote the products or services of a company that does infringe. Given that the Internet is nothing if not a vast bazaar of hyperlinked, cross-promoted Web sites, this could become a problem of rather staggering proportions.

Imagine, for example, that your firm is among the 250,000 members of Amazon.com's "associates program," under which Amazon pays to its affiliated sites a bounty of between 7 and 15 percent of any book or video sold to customers that they refer. Now imagine further that Amazon is one day sued for patent infringement—not an impossibility, considering that the company has already been sued for theft of trade secrets. In such an event, you could receive not a bounty for your promotional help, but a summons to a multimillion-dollar patent suit.

Amazon.com is hardly the only e-commerce venture with this sort of cross-promotional "associates" program. Hundreds of other e-commerce concerns run similar programs, including the on-line music retailer CDNow, which has 207,000 members in its own stable of affiliates. So widespread has the practice become, in fact, that the *New York Times* recently suggested that "1999 may be the Year of the Affiliate, as Web merchants realize that one way to balance the books is to recruit other sites to help sell their goods."[14] The *Times* did not, however, mention that it may also be a good way to devastate the balance sheets of quite a few affiliated Web businesses with one colossal contributory-infringement suit.

THE OPEN SOURCE CHALLENGE

It is precisely Net patents' enhanced power (and threat) that has Open Source developers such as Bruce Perens so worried. They are especially concerned about the growing proliferation of Internet trash patents that don't really cover unique new inventions but, having been granted by overworked and under-experienced government patent examiners anyway, are now being used by Internet carpetbaggers to intimidate competitors or extort money from businesses fearful of the exorbitant costs of defending against a patent suit.

"The quandary for us," says Perens, "is whether we should assemble a pool of our own patents for self-defense, or instead just go out and bust some of these trash patents."

This is no idle threat, as a company called Wang Global discovered in the spring of 1998. Wang had sued the Netscape Corporation (since acquired by America Online) for patent infringement, claiming that because Netscape's Web browser lets users save and rename Web pages to their hard drives using the "Save As" command, it infringed Wang's patents. What so outraged Netscape and many others, however, was the fact that Wang's 15-year-old patents actually dealt with the technology of videotext, an entirely different (and now defunct) medium. Thus on April 24, 1998, when Netscape issued a call for help in fighting the suit (two months after the company had won praise from freeware developers for making Navigator's source code public), the Open Source community responded in force. Programmers from around the world began scouring old programming journals and databases, searching for prior-art citations that might prove that the techniques Wang claimed it had invented in the early 1980s actually existed in the public domain prior to Wang's patents, thus invalidating them. The freeware detectives apparently located hundreds of relevant prior-art citations, although whether the judge's decision two weeks later to dismiss all of Wang's patent claims was based on that newly discovered prior art or the result of problems with the claim language of the patents themselves is not clear.

Just over a year later, a similar patent-busting effort was launched against a company called Intermind that threatened to assert its patent for technology that gives consumers more control over information collected from them as they surf the Web. On May 3, 1999, the Web's leading standards body—the World Wide Web Consortium—issued a call for developers around the world to search for prior-art references that might invalidate Intermind's patent threat.

Both incidents demonstrated the collective power of Net developers, as well as the dangers of threatening them (or their friends) with what they feel are extortionist patent claims. As one very happy Netscape official boasted after the Wang suit was tossed, "If you're going to file a bogus patent claim, know that you're going up against a whole community of Net developers."[15]

And not just *any* community of developers, either. For Open Source programmers are not just a bunch of software hippies out in the cyber-hinterlands, growing their own code and home-spinning their gossamer threads of software far from the madding crush of real-world business. On the contrary, they are some of the very best software designers on the planet. In fact, their software pretty much runs the planet, or at least the planetwide communications network we call the Internet. They may be an iconoclastic and even somewhat motley crew, but without them there wouldn't even be an Internet for companies such as Wang to lust over.

Take Brian Behlendorf. He and his ad hoc team of co-developers created the Apache program that runs the majority of Internet servers in the world today, enabling these to simultaneously feed text, sound, and images to tens of millions of Net surfers. Or developer Eric Allman, whose Sendmail program routes up to 80 percent of all e-mail messages on the Internet—and successfully delivers hundreds of millions of pieces of e-mail each day without a hitch (unlike a certain off-line postal system we know). Then there's Paul Vixie, lead developer of the Bind program that makes it possible to type word-based rather than numeric Internet addresses to guide us to our on-line destinations—"WhiteHouse.gov" instead of 198.137.241.30, for example, or "Sex.com" instead of 209.132.88.50. And don't forget Larry Wall, creator of the Perl scripting language that enables Web sites to respond interactively to user requests—in other words, it helps make e-commerce possible.

Indeed, the Internet itself, including the World Wide Web and the software for browsing it, is basically freeware. Freeware that may have been jerry-built and patched together out of the detritus of university graduate research projects and all-night hacker coding frenzies, perhaps, but a marvel of software engineering nonetheless. Imagine a sort of virtual Manhattan Project—only one in which all secrets are shared and the critical components are scrounged up at garage sales—and you get a sense of just how extraordinary Open Source's achievement is.

A New Model of Innovation

It is not only extraordinary; it's also unprecedented. During previous industrial emergences throughout history, initial invention activity was conducted either cottage industry–style—that is, by inventors driven by a passion to invent, such as today's Open Source developers—or through scientific and university research labs. Knowledge was shared freely among inventors and intellectual property played only a minor role in the innovation process.

But at a certain point, when innovation began to give rise to significant commercial activity, patenting has always supplanted cottage industry invention as the chief platform for innovation. As one study of late nineteenth- and early twentieth-century inventors noted, "the channels of information [surrounding] the patent system worked effectively to diffuse technological knowledge." [16] These channels included the PTO as well as publications such as *Scientific American* that printed details of all the most important new patents.

On the Internet, however, the cottage industry–style sharing of ideas represented by the Open Source movement has continued to serve as an important force for innovation well into the commercialization phase of the medium. Nothing like this has ever happened before, and it is doubtless the result of the collective power and inventive effectiveness that the interconnected Net has given to otherwise isolated and poorly funded independent software developers.

According to Open Source leader Eric Raymond, whose widely read 1997 treatise, *The Cathedral and the Bazaar,* articulates the economic and philosophical basis for the Open Source movement, this collective inventive power results in software that is often superior to that built by conventional patent-driven research efforts. "If your source [code] is open, you get peer review, you get reliability," he told Andrew Leonard, the senior technology writer for the on-line magazine *Salon.* "The four most critical pieces of infrastructure that make the Internet work—*Bind, Perl, Sendmail* and *Apache*—every one of these is Open Source, and every one is super reliable. The Internet would not function if they weren't super reliable, and they are super reliable precisely because throughout their entire history people have been constantly banging on the code, looking at the source, seeing what breaks and fixing it." [17]

Salon's Leonard, one of the most informed observers of the Open Source scene, agrees: "The complexities of some of these large software projects are so great now that really the only way you can pull them off is through the efforts of huge distributed collectives," he believes. "The Internet is unique in that it enables a kind of 'linked mind' approach to software development, and this is what Open Source has been able to harness."

Even Microsoft, the company most threatened by Open

Source's Linux operating system, agrees that the Open Source approach has advantages. Or so it would appear from a reading of two extraordinary internal Microsoft memos that were leaked to Open Source leader Eric Raymond in late 1998. Dubbed the Halloween 1 and 2 Documents because Raymond posted them on the Web October 31 and November 3, 1998—and later confirmed as authentic by Microsoft—the memos were written by two Microsoft engineers to assess the danger posed by Linux and the Open Source movement. What is so striking about these memos is their frank admission of the superiority of Open Source software (OSS) in several key respects.

"Rapid creation and deployment of incremental [improvements] and bug fixes [combined with] greater code inspection and debugging in OSS software results in higher-quality code than commercial [e.g., Microsoft] software," concede the memos. What's more, "because the pool of potential OSS developers is massive, it is economically viable [for them] to simultaneously investigate multiple solutions to a problem and choose the best solution in the end." In fact, say the authors, "The ability of OSS to collect and harness the collective IQ of thousands of individuals across the Internet is simply amazing."[18]

But while this collaborative approach clearly has its merits from an engineering standpoint, can any development approach based on giving away your most valuable asset—that is, your intellectual property—really succeed *as a business* in today's hypercompetitive Internet?

To some extent, it already has. Over the past year, software industry leaders such as IBM, Oracle, Netscape, Apple, Novell, Corel, and many others have all either opened up portions of their software code for Open Source developers to tinker with or have customized versions of their own programs to run on the Linux operating system. Moreover, hardware companies such as Hewlett-Packard, Silicon Graphics, Sun Microsystems, Compaq,

Dell, and IBM have begun offering the Linux operating system as an alternative to Microsoft's Windows NT on certain of their high-end computer and Internet server product lines.

One of the most important of these Linux deals was announced in mid-February 1999, when IBM decided to offer Linux on its Netfinity line of Intel-based servers as well as on its PC 300 commercial desktop PCs, IntelliStation workstations, and ThinkPad notebook computers. IBM had previously announced its support for Apache, another Open Source program. "A lot of companies are running Linux on some server in a closet somewhere," says Giga Information Group analyst Stacey Quandt. "But when IBM comes out and says they're supporting it, it creates a lot more credibility."[19]

As Brian Sanders, brand manager for IBM's Netfinity line, explained it, "Linux is quite a phenomenon. It's taken us somewhat by surprise that it has grown so substantially in such a short period of time."[20] The best estimates put the total number of Linux users at somewhere between 10 and 15 million as of early 1999. And according to the market research firm International Data Corporation, Linux market share had already topped 17 percent by early 1999, nearly half of Windows NT's 36 percent share of the market.

Linux's appeal does not stem solely from its price (or lack thereof). For users, the software's high reliability, ease of customization, and capacity to run on a wide variety of hardware platforms are also important incentives. And for industry leaders such as IBM and Hewlett-Packard, support for Open Source is likewise not just a matter of exploiting a new market opportunity. It also offers a way to potentially blunt Microsoft's hegemony and bolster their own negotiating posture vis-à-vis the "Beast of Redmond" (as Microsoft is less-than-affectionately known).

"From a corporate standpoint, everybody in the business sees this in part as a flanking maneuver against Microsoft," explains *Salon*'s Leonard. "Finally, there's an alternative. There's another force in the marketplace now."

The Limitations of Open Source

It would be a serious mistake, however, to expect the downfall of Microsoft any time soon—remember similar predictions in the heady early days of Netscape's Internet browser? The fact is that Linux's growth is still concentrated mainly among small and mid-sized enterprises, universities, and research institutions, as well as in such second-tier corporate applications as delivering Web pages over company intranets. With few trusted, brand-name Linux support vendors, not to mention a dearth of experience running Linux on large mission-critical corporate systems, Fortune 500 companies will certainly be cautious in choosing Linux over Windows NT.

The Open Source approach also has several intrinsic weaknesses, as Microsoft's infamous Halloween memos point out. These include a "piecemeal approach [that] will make it especially hard to solve [fundamental] architectural problems" in the software, and "difficulty in starting [or] sustaining" a truly innovative project, as opposed to simply enhancing product features. The memos even quote Raymond's *The Cathedral and the Bazaar:* "One can test, debug and improve in bazaar [or Open Source] style, but it would be very hard to *originate* a project in [Open Source] mode."[21]

Another weakness is the inherent fragmentation of Open Source development, which may lead to a multiplicity of incompatible versions of Linux—a problem that has plagued the Unix operating system, from which Linux is derived, for over 15 years. The anarchic nature of the Open Source movement itself exacerbates the risk of fragmentation and "code forking," in which different groups of programmers take the software down differing and incompatible roads. Even Netscape, the first major firm to open up its source code and embrace the freeware model, acknowledged this danger in a recent Securities and Exchange Commission filing when it noted that "the free source code [to Netscape's Internet browser] may lead to a proliferation of incompatible or competitive products, potentially creating brand and market confusion."

Can Open Source Survive?

The biggest challenge facing Open Source developers and businesses, however, may come from the outside. As the Halloween memos ominously warn, "The effect of patents and copyright in combating Linux remains to be investigated."

The ultimate winners in the e-commerce wars may be determined by a patent shoot-out.

There it is: the patent bludgeon! And make no mistake, patents are fully capable of crippling Open Source development to the point where it is no longer competitive with advances in proprietary software. Hackers may cry about "freedom" and complain all they like about "corporate bean counters" taking away their "right" to appropriate others' patented technology, but they are doomed to eventual irrelevancy unless they come up with a strategy for dealing with the irreversible fact that patents are on the Net to stay.

Indeed, if history is any guide, the power of these patents to determine the winners and losers of Internet business competition will likely only grow stronger. History shows that once the initial race to innovate and grab market share in an emerging new industry has been superseded by a period of shakeouts and consolidation in which firms with the most successful business models contend with one another for market dominance—precisely the period we are now entering in the life cycle of the Internet e-commerce sector—patents then often become decisive. As one observer of the history of U.S. patenting has noted, "The ultimate winner in the race to capture the lead position in a new industry is often determined by the outcome of a patent shoot-out." [22]

Bruce Perens himself seemed to recognize this "patent reality" in a November 1998 white paper he wrote entitled "Preparing for the Coming Intellectual Property Offensive." Correctly noting that "patents may be the ground on which the Open Source battle is won or lost," Perens proposed that free software developers "fund the development of [their own] patentable ideas" both to cross-license defensively against infringement claims and to bolster Open Source efforts to "maintain a technological lead" in Internet software development efforts. [23]

The potential for Open Source developers to leverage patent realities to their advantage may be even greater than Perens realizes, however. For by tapping the strategic power of patents—and by using the interlinked Net economy to organize their movement more effectively—Open Source developers may be able to accomplish much more than simply ensure their survival. They may also be able to significantly increase their power and success and eliminate (or at least greatly reduce) the threat they face from both patents in general and trash patents in particular.

Trash Patent Bin. Open Source developers could, for example, simply build upon their Wang and Intermind experiences to take the lead in establishing a central repository of patent and nonpatent prior art—a *Trash Patent Bin,* if you will. Any company hit with a patent infringement claim or demand for licensing fees could search the Trash Patent Bin for prior art and gather the evidence needed (if it exists) to defend itself. Indeed, the mere existence of a Trash Patent Bin database would reduce the incentives for initiating extortionist patent claims in the first place.

Interestingly, a senior official of the U.S. Patent and Trademark Office—he insisted on remaining anonymous for now— heartily endorsed such an Open Source–led effort to create a Trash Patent Bin database of prior art. "It would make our jobs a lot easier because right now we simply don't have the resources or capabilities to do as good a job in prior art examinations as we would like on some of these patents," the PTO official declared. "Our examiners could certainly make use of it. We might even require applicants to search it before submitting their applications. I think the Trash Patent Bin would benefit everyone."

The beauty of the Trash Patent Bin concept is that it is based on one simple and inarguable premise: if a patent can be invalidated, then it *should* be invalidated. Valid patents would not be threatened by a prior-art database, because they presumably cover truly novel inventions for which no invalidating prior art would exist. And as for those holding poorly researched or otherwise invalid patents, they would certainly think twice before asserting claims against innocent inventors and businesses.

An Independent Inventor's Market. Bruce Perens's suggestion that Open Source developers cultivate their own portfolio of patents raises another intriguing opportunity: the creation of an Open Source–led marketplace where independent inventors could market and license their inventions. Such an independent inventor's market would obviously serve as a useful financing tool for Open Source developers and their organizations. But it could also stimulate the contribution by commercial firms of some of their intellectual property in exchange either for already-developed software technology or as barter-for-hire for teams of

Open Source programmers who could help them with their software debugging and other development efforts—an "Open Source Development Corps," if you will.

There is some historical precedent for an independent inventor's market. Prior to the mid-1920s, in fact, the corporate R&D department did not even exist—at least not in its current form as an organized unit for the in-house development of new technology. Rather, what we now call the corporate R&D department actually functioned as a business development unit that scouted for externally generated inventions, which were then licensed from independent inventors and brought in-house to be developed into products. It was only in the 1930s, with the growing complexity of technology and the rising human and capital costs of invention, that the modern-day system of in-house corporate R&D came to dominate the field of invention.

It is interesting to note that this independent inventor's market also had the effect of strengthening the rights of inventors who worked as employees within firms. It wasn't until the 1930s, in fact, that companies began to routinely appropriate the patent rights of employees as they do today. Prior to then, "inventors hotly contested firms' assertions that they deserved such ownership rights, and the courts typically backed inventors over their employers." [24]

But now, the same interlinked Net architecture that gives Open Source and other independent developers their collective power once again makes this sort of independent inventor's market possible. Indeed, the first efforts toward organizing and harnessing the whirlwind of independent innovation on the Net are already under way through services such as PatentAuction.com and the IPMarketPlace, which plan to auction the patented or copyrighted technologies of independent inventors. As for the notion of creating teams of rapid-deployment Open Source commandos to help firms with their software development and debugging efforts, services such as OpenAvenue, SourceXChange, and the Free Software Bazaar have already begun serving as middlemen between mainstream firms and on-call freelance developers.

Regardless of whether or not independent developers choose to embrace the idea of a Trash Patent Bin or an Independent Inventors Market, the point here is that the growing power of Internet patents represents not just a threat to the Open Source community but a major opportunity as well. For just as money can buy a person freedom from the rat race of materialistic pursuit, so might the wise use of patents' enable Open Source developers to continue pursuing their unique style of patent-free software innovation.

PATENT GUIDELINES FOR E-COMMERCE SUCCESS

However Open Source developers choose to confront today's patent realities, their extraordinary success to date reminds us that the e-commerce marketplace presents some unique new challenges for businesses. Among these is the fact that competitive barriers are collapsing all across the Internet, increasing by orders of magnitude both the opportunities as well as the dangers that companies face today. At the same time, a power shift in the center of gravity of technology and business innovation has given small start-ups and independent inventors a new economic potency and eliminated many of the competitive advantages previously enjoyed only by large capital-rich enterprises. As a result, it is no longer capital or other traditional inputs but innovative ideas—whether manifested in new technologies, new business models, or new methods for

Unless you patent your core advantage, you risk becoming another "Dot.com DOA."

serving customers—that have become the key factors in e-commerce success today.

In this new environment, the challenge of using intellectual property as a strategic weapon in business competition has taken on new and critical importance in corporate leadership circles. No simple formula, of course, could possibly capture all the complex and still-evolving facets of an effective Internet patent strategy. But we can point to a few key pillars of such a strategy, and show how these may enhance a company's prospects for e-commerce success.

Establish a Proprietary Market Position

- *Protect your core product or service advantage.* With competitive barriers collapsing, your best defense against bigger or more powerful rivals may be to patent and protect the key proprietary technologies and business methods that give your products and services their value-added competitive edge over those of competitors.

- *Enhance your brand clout.* Along with a proprietary product advantage, branding is your next best guarantee of success. Employ the IP3 for R&D strategy (see Chapter 4) to protect, enhance, and communicate more effectively the key brand-differentiating features of your product or service to consumers.

Bolster Your E-Commerce Competitiveness

- *Tap the power of Open Source.* To achieve ubiquity or establish your technology as an industry standard, take the Open Source approach and offer royalty-free licenses (while reserving your rights to any proprietary future upgrades). And when time to market is critical, the speed and quality-control benefits of the Open Source approach may offer just the edge you need over competitors.

- *Reduce your risk.* Employ "patent mapping" to steer your R&D and M&A programs around infringement and due diligence potholes. Also avoid the contributory infringement dangers intrinsic to the interlinked Net by indemnifying yourself from any liability incurred by vendors, suppliers, or partners. Small firms should consider patent insurance that pays the legal costs of action against bigger rivals.

Leverage the Increased Value of Ideas

- *Use IP assets to bolster financing and valuation efforts.* Audit and value your patent assets to help secure equity or debt financing, as well as to help establish a higher market valuation for your firm.

- *Mine unused patents for revenue gold.* If you have strong patents on nonstrategic (to you) technologies or business methods that others would find valuable, establish a licensing program to generate incremental revenues.

FINAL THOUGHTS

In mid-July 1999, as this book was going to press, Internet newswires began to hum with the startling announcement by a company called Audiohighway.com that it had been issued a patent it claimed entitled the company to "ownership" of the entire on-line digital music industry.[25] Suspicions were immediately raised about the validity and defensibility of the patent, however, because it apparently cited no prior art whatsoever. Will Audiohighway's bold grab for a hefty chunk of on-line music industry revenues ultimately fail, just as similar Internet patent threats from Wang and Sightsound were torpedoed by prior art and claims challenges? Or could this be a patent that leads to the birth of a new twenty-first century business dynasty, much as

Chester Carlson's original xerography patent served as the foundation of Xerox's twentieth-century success?

No one yet knows the answer to that question. What can be said with absolute assurance, however, is that patent-driven business wars are soon going to be commonplace on the Net. And it will be the wise e-commerce executive who prepares for these coming patent wars now.

Still, it remains unclear precisely how important patents will prove to be in shaping the dynamics of competition on the Net. To judge from previous industrial history, they could be very important. But history is not everything, as the unprecedented success of the Open Source movement demonstrates. Nonetheless, it is probably safe to conclude that in at least a few key sectors of the Internet economy, intellectual property will ultimately be decisive in determining the winners and losers of tomorrow's e-commerce competition.

We must stress once again, however, that patent strategy is no Holy Grail for automatic business success—especially not on the Internet. E-commerce is still an industry in the making, after all, and the best strategies will have to be developed through trial and error. At this point in the Net's development, business strategies—even patent-savvy ones—can only serve as rough outlines, guesses about the path to value extraction. It's all uncharted territory.

The wonderful thing about intellectual property, however, is the trail of competitive intelligence it leaves in its wake concerning the shape and direction of corporate strategy. If the e-commerce landscape is indeed still uncharted territory, then patents are footprints left along the frontier—valuable guides to those who know how to read them.

And especially valuable to those who know how to *use* them. For in a world where knowledge really is power, patents will be the "smart" bombs of tomorrow's business wars.

NOTES

1 The New Competitive Battlefield

1. Thomas E. Weber, *The Wall Street Journal*, 1 April 1999.
2. Sabra Chartrand, "Patents," *The New York Times*, 5 April 1999.
3. Jakob Nielsen, "Web Patent Bonanza," *Alertbox*, 27 December 1998, <http://www.useit.com/alertbox/>.
4. Jeffrey Young, "Inventing Money," *Forbes Digital Tool*, 9 February 1998, <http//:www.forbes.com>.
5. Amy Rogers, "Sun Explains Role in AOL-Netscape Pact," *Computer Reseller News*, 24 November 1998.
6. "The Sun Story Is Increasingly about Future Potential," *Dow Jones News/Retrieval*, 10 December 1998.
7. Young, "Inventing Money."
8. Masako Fukuda, "Lost Sales Prod Japan to Spread Gospel of Intellectual Property Law," *The Nikkei Weekly*, 2 November 1998.
9. Takeshi Isayama, keynote address at the annual meeting of the Intellectual Property Owners (IPO), San Francisco, Calif., 16 November 1998.
10. Jim Landers, "Japanese Finally Getting Tough about Protecting Products," *Dallas Morning News*, 28 September 1998.
11. Leigh Buchanan, "Face-to-Face: Walker Digital's Jay Walker," *Inc.*, November 1998.

12. Marianne Nardone, "First Patent Securitization Pending," *Bondweek, a publication of Institutional Investor,* 18 January 1999.

13. See http://www.iqpc.com.

14. Teresa Riordan, "New Technology Revives Old Debate," *The New York Times,* 4 January 1999.

15. William T. Ellis and Aaron C. Chatterjee, "Patent Wars Come to Wall Street," *IP Magazine,* November 1998.

16. Coopers & Lybrand, "Maximizing the Value of Intellectual Property" (brochure, 1997).

17. The Delphi Group, "Delphi Group Research Identifies Leading Business Applications of Knowledge Management" (press release, 29 March 1999).

18. PriceWaterhouseCoopers, "Doubling of Patent/Trademark Issuances Heralds Golden Age of Property" (press release, 26 March 1999).

19. Rusty Cawley, "Summit to Offer Protection in Patent Infringement Cases," *Dallas Business Journal,* 11 January 1999.

20. Sherry Eng, "10 Hot Jobs in Silicon Valley," *San Jose Mercury News,* 5 January 1999.

21. Samuel Kortum and Joshua Lerner, "Stronger Protection or Technological Revolution: What's Behind the Recent Surge in Patenting?" working paper 98-012, Harvard Business School, Boston, Mass., 1997.

22. Gregory Aharonian, *Internet Patent News Service,* <http://www.patents@world.std.com>.

23. Ibid.

24. Scott Thurm, "A Flood of New Patents Stirs Up a Dispute over Tactics," *The Wall Street Journal,* 9 October 1998.

25. Seth Shulman, *Owning the Future: Inside the Battles to Control the New Assets—Genes, Software, Databases, and Technological Know-How—That Make Up the Lifeblood of the New Economy* (Boston: Houghton Mifflin, 1999), 3.

26. Mike France, "Patent Nonsense," *Business Week,* 12 April 1999.

27. Shulman, *Owning the Future,* 52–53.

28. Victoria Slind-For, "Cellpro Judge Criticizes Lawyers, Venture Capitalists," *National Law Journal,* 11 August 1997.

29. Ibid.

30. Shulman, *Owning the Future,* 17.

31. See http://www.nber.org.

32. Naomi R. Lamoreaux and Kenneth L. Sokoloff, "Inventors, Firms, and

the Market for Technology: U.S. Manufacturing in the Late Nineteenth and Early Twentieth Centuries," Historical Paper 98, National Bureau of Economic Research, Cambridge, Mass., 1997.

33. Adam B. Jaffe and Josh Lerner, "Privatizing R&D: Patent Policy and the Commercialization of National Laboratory Technologies," working paper 7064, National Bureau of Economic Research, Cambridge, Mass., 1999.

34. Jonathan Eaton and Samuel Kortum, "Trade in Ideas: Patenting and Productivity in the OECD," working paper 5049, National Bureau of Economic Research, Cambridge, Mass., 1995.

35. Robert J. Barro and Xavier Sala-I-Martin, "Technology Diffusion, Convergence, and Growth," working paper 5151, National Bureau of Economic Research, Cambridge, Mass., 1995.

2 Restoring the Lost Art of Patent Strategy

1. Andrew E. Serwer, "Michael Dell Turns the PC World Inside Out," *Fortune,* 8 September 1997.

2. Marcia Stepanek, "What Does No. 1 Do for an Encore?" *Business Week,* 2 November 1998.

3. Michael Kanellos, "Compaq Aims for Direct Hit," *CNET News.Com,* 30 October 1998, <http://www.news.com/>.

4. Takeshi Isayama, keynote address at the annual meeting of the Intellectual Property Owners (IPO), San Francisco, Calif., 16 November 1998.

5. Kate Thomas, "Oil Biz Gushes Patents," *National Law Journal,* 16 February 1998.

6. Stephen C. Glazier, *Patent Strategies for Business,* 3rd ed. (Washington, D.C.: Law & Business Institute, 1997), 164.

7. Jeffrey Young, "Inventing Money," *Forbes Digital Tool,* 9 February 1998, <http://www.forbes.com>.

8. Teresa Riordan, "New Technology Revives Old Debate," *The New York Times,* 4 January 1999.

9. Bronwyn H. Hall and Rose Marie Ham, "The Patent Paradox Revisited: Determinants of Patenting in the US Semiconductor Industry," working paper 7062, National Bureau of Economic Research, Cambridge, Mass., 1999.

10. Ibid.

11. Josh Lerner, "Patenting in the Shadow of Competitors," *Journal of Law and Economics* 38, no. 2 (October 1995).

12. Bill Gates memo.

13. Erik Espe, "Friendlier Courts, Higher Stakes Unleash Patent Suits," *The Business Journal of San Jose,* 5 July 1999.

14. Richard Korman, "Lo! Here Come the Technology Patents. Lo! Here Come the Lawsuits,"*The New York Times,* 27 December 1998.

15. Ibid.

16. Ibid.

17. John Brooks, *Telephone: The First Hundred Years* (New York: Harper & Row, 1975), 80.

18. Samuel Kortum and Joshua Lerner, "Stronger Protection or Technological Revolution: What's Behind the Recent Surge in Patenting?" working paper 98-012, Harvard Business School, Boston, Mass., 1997.

19. Randy Myers, "Getting a Grip on Intangibles," *CFO,* September 1996.

20. Bernard Condon, "Gaps in GAAP," *Forbes,* 25 January 1999.

21. Coopers & Lybrand, "Maximizing the Value of Intellectual Property" (brochure, 1997).

22. Thomas A. Stewart, "Intellectual Capital: Your Company's Most Valuable Asset," *Fortune,* 3 October 1994.

23. Lester C. Thurow, "Needed: A New System of Intellectual Property Rights," *Harvard Business Review,* September–October 1997.

24. David J. Teece, "Capturing Value From Knowledge Assets: The New Economy, Markets for Know-How, and Intangible Assets," *California Management Review,* 1 April 1998.

3 The New CEO Challenge

1. Douglas K. Smith and Robert C. Alexander, *Fumbling the Future: How Xerox Invented Then Ignored the First Personal Computer* (New York: William Morrow and Company, 1988).

2. Xerox subsequently engineered a 2-for-1 stock split.

3. Based on Xerox's forward-looking price-to-earnings ratio of 80 at the time of this writing.

4. Since this interview was conducted, Paul Germeraad has joined

7. Fred Warshofsky, *The Patent Wars: The Battle to Own the World's Technology* (New York: John Wiley & Sons, 1994), 111, 123.

8. Irving Rappaport is now vice president of intellectual property at Aurigin Systems, whose CEO is Kevin Rivette, one of the authors of this book.

9. Randy Myers, "Fighting Words: Growing Ranks of Litigants Are Putting Price Tags on Ideas," *CFO*, March 1998.

10. Aman, "Money of Invention."

11. Warshofsky, *Patent Wars*, 18.

12. Steven Lipin, "British Firm with Piles of Patents Does Best to Hustle for Licenses," *The Wall Street Journal*, 9 November 1998.

13. Barry Nelson, "Tech Firm Has Big Mission," *Calgary Herald*, 2 May 1999.

14. Mark Schankerman, "How Valuable Is Patent Protection? Estimates by Technology Field," *RAND Journal of Economics* 29, no. 1 (Spring 1998).

15. Thomas A. Stewart, "Trying to Grasp the Intangible," *Fortune*, 2 October 1995.

16. Jeffrey Young, "Inventing Money," *Forbes Digital Tool*, 9 February 1998, <http://www.forbes.com>.

17. Marianne Nardone, "First Patent Securitization Pending," *Bondweek, a publication of Institutional Investor*, 18 January 1999.

18. Scott Thurm, "A Flood of New Web Patents Stirs Up a Dispute Over Tactics," *The Wall Street Journal*, 9 October 1998.

19. Richard Brandt, "Instapreneur!" *Upside*, 21 January 1999.

20. Juan Hovey, "Intellectual Property Can Take Business to Next Level," *Los Angeles Times*, 10 February 1999.

21. Juan Hovey, "Value of Intellectual Property Can Be Key to More Funds," *Los Angeles Times*, 17 February 1999.

22. Ibid.

23. Justin Hibbard, "Protecting Innovation," *Information Week*, 22 February 1999.

24. *The Intellectual Capital Monitor: Patents and Performance* (New Britain, Penn.), March 1999.

25. "Outlook: A Novel Investment Strategy," *Forbes Digital Tool*, 27 July 1999, <http://www.forbes.com>.

26. Young, "Inventing Money."

6 Patent Mapping Your Business Development Strategy

1. Carol Wilson, "TI Turns ADSL Industry on Its Ear," *Interactive Week*, 24 November 1997.
2. Carol Wilson, "ADSL Pioneers Amati, Westell Agree to Merge," *Interactive Week*, 1 October 1997.
3. Ibid.
4. Saul Hansell, "The Small Get Big and the Big Get Bigger," *The New York Times*, 4 January 1999.
5. Richard Teitelbaum, "Mergers, Mergers Everywhere, But Do Shareholders Benefit?" *The New York Times*, 29 November 1998.
6. Ronald Henkoff and Amy R. Kover, "Growing Your Company: Five Ways to Do It Right," *Fortune*, 25 November 1996.
7. Whit Andrews, "Firefly Is Bought by Microsoft," *Internet World*, 13 April 1998, <http://internetworld.com>.
8. Herb Greenberg, "Stent Mania: Is Guidant Corp. Secretly After EVT's Patent?" *San Francisco Chronicle*, 8 October 1997.
9. Louis Hau, "Bidding for Pfizer Unit Pressures Potential Buyers' Shares," *The Wall Street Journal*, 29 May 1998.
10. Tim Stevens, "Multiplication by Addition," *Industry Week*, 1 July 1996.
11. Fred Warshofsky, *The Patent Wars: The Battle to Own the World's Technology* (New York: John Wiley & Sons, 1994), 18.
12. Joseph B. Cahill, "Closing Plants Zenith's Only Survival Hope," *Crain's Chicago Business*, 6 April 1998.
13. Josh Kosman, "Buyout Firms Undervalue Intellectual Property," *Buyouts*, 22 March 1999.
14. Ibid.
15. Ibid.
16. Ibid.
17. Larry Kahaner, *Competitive Intelligence* (New York: Simon & Schuster, 1996), 141.

7 Surviving the Internet Patent Wars

1. Dyan Machan, "An Edison for a New Age?" *Forbes*, 17 May 1999.
2. Justin Hibbard, "Protecting Innovation," *Information Week*, 22 February 1999.

3. Thomas E. Weber and Scott Thurm, "Priceline.com Indicates Its Planned IPO Could Place Market Value at $1 Billion," *The Wall Street Journal,* 19 March 1999.

4. Bloomberg News, "Priceline Receives Another Patent," *CNET News.Com,* 7 May 1999, <http://www.news.com/>.

5. Machan, "Edison."

6. Beth Lipton, "Floodgates Open for Patent Cases," *CNET News.Com.,* 28 August 1998, <http://www.news.com/>.

7. John S. McClenahen, "Net Gains," *Industry Week,* 17 May 1999.

8. Steve Hamm and Marcia Stepanek, "From Reengineering to E-Engineering," *Business Week,* 22 March 1999.

9. Hibbard, "Protecting Innovation."

10. H. Garrett DeYoung, "Thieves Among Us: If Knowledge Is Your Most Valuable Asset, Why Is It So Easily Stolen?" *Industry Week,* 17 June 1996.

11. DeYoung, "Thieves."

12. Ibid.

13. Bloomberg News, "NES Sues eBay, Alleges Patent Infringement," *CNET News.Com,* 23 March 1999, <http://www.news.com/>.

14. Bob Tedeschi, "E-Commerce Report," *The New York Times,* 22 March 1999.

15. Paul Festa, "Netscape Recruits Mozilla in Suit," *CNET News.Com,* 24 April 1998, <http://www.news.com/>.

16. Naomi R. Lamoreaux and Kenneth L. Sokoloff, "Inventors, Firms, and the Market for Technology: U.S. Manufacturing in the Late Nineteenth and Early Twentieth Centuries," Historical Paper 98, National Bureau of Economic Research, Cambridge, Mass., 1997.

17. Andrew Leonard, "Let My Software Go," *Salon,* 14 April 1998. <http://www.salonmagazine.com/>.

18. The Halloween Documents, <http://www.opensource.org/halloween>.

19. Amy Harmon, "IBM to Offer Linux with Netfinity Computers," *The New York Times,* 18 February 1999.

20. Stephen Shankland, "Computing Heavyweights Warm to Linux," *CNET News.Com,* 27 January 1999, <http://www.news.com/>.

21. Eric Raymond, *The Cathedral and the Bazaar,* quoted in Halloween Documents.

22. Stephen C. Glazier, *Patent Strategies for Business,* 3rd ed. (Washington, D.C.: Law & Business Institute, 1997), 158.

23. Bruce Perens, "Preparing for the Coming Intellectual Property Offensive," <http://www.linuxworld/lw-1988-11/lw-11-thesource.html>.

24. Lamoreaux and Sokoloff, "Inventors, Firms."

25. Oscar S. Cisneros, "Audiohighway: We Own Net Music," *Wired News*, 14 July 1999.

INDEX

ABOUT THE AUTHORS

Kevin G. Rivette (kevin_rivette@aurigin.com) is co-founder and chairman of Aurigin Systems, Inc., which develops intellectual property management solutions. A former patent attorney, he is a frequent speaker on patent strategy issues.

David Kline (dkline@well.com) is a business strategy consultant specializing in patent strategy and e-commerce-related business opportunities. A commentator on public radio's *Marketplace* program, he is also the author of *Road Warriors*.

The authors' ongoing analysis of timely patent strategy issues is available at www.rembrandtsintheattic.com.